Rethinking Community Research

David Studdert • Valerie Walkerdine

Rethinking Community Research

Inter-relationality, Communal Being and Commonality

David Studdert
School of Social Sciences
Cardiff University
Cardiff, United Kingdom

Valerie Walkerdine
School of Social Sciences
Cardiff University
Cardiff, United Kingdom

ISBN 978-1-137-51452-3 (hardcover)   ISBN 978-1-137-51453-0   (eBook)
ISBN 978-1-349-70312-8 (softcover)
DOI 10.1057/978-1-137-51453-0

Library of Congress Control Number: 2016948414

This Palgrave Macmillan imprint is published by Springer Nature
The registered company is Macmillan Publishers Ltd. London

We dedicate this book absolutely and wholeheartedly to the wonderful people of Market-Town who exemplified communal being-ness and held out for us the possibility of experiencing and understanding just what it might mean. To their generosity and kindness. There are particular people who helped us a great deal and whom we cannot name because of our need to protect the anonymity of the town, but they know who they are and we thank them from the bottom of our hearts.

Acknowledgements

We must acknowledge first and foremost the people of Market-Town to whom we have dedicated the book.

Many people from that town were part of the projects that we organised. These projects were funded by the Arts and Humanities Research Council Connected Communities (AHRC) and Cultural Value programmes, and we gratefully acknowledge their support for the following grants, out of which this book grew.

For some of those grants, other co-investigators were an essential part of the project teams: Graham Crow, Niamh Moore, Ian Hargreaves and Sally Mackey. For their considerable input, we remain incredibly grateful. They are not, however, responsible for the writing and views presented in this volume, for which the authors take full responsibility. We should also thank Keri Facer and the Connected Communities team. Keri was indefatigable in support of the work of this programme, and she contributed a great deal to making it as good a programme as it was. The staff of the AHRC section devoted to this programme should also be mentioned in gratitude for their always helpful and supportive presence.

Both authors would also like to thank the School of Social Sciences at Cardiff University, who have been unfailingly supportive of our commitment to research and to this trajectory of work in particular. There has been generosity of spirit which has been really appreciated.

Contents

Introduction

Sue has just posted a photo of an old open-air swimming pool that was shut down by the local council in the 1990s on a Facebook page designed to explore local history and memories of a British market town. Within minutes, six excited comments have appeared about this pool and the good times had there and the photo has been shared over 100 times.

In this volume, we take the reader to this town in order to approach afresh the way in which we think about and research 'community'. As we show, 'community' has become a term both constantly used by policy-makers and at the same time just as vehemently derided by academics. We consider that this position serves no one but can be approached differently, that is, by understanding what community is in a different way. The basis of that different way was set out in an earlier volume (Studdert, 2006), in which, with the help of the work of Hannah Arendt, Studdert outlined a way beyond a set of impasses around our understandings of community. In this volume, we take this approach further by developing an analytic that allows us to investigate community in a new and different way, and we put that analytic to work in the streets of a town we call Market-Town, a smallish town, like many towns in Britain and all over the world, in which we conducted three research projects.

This monograph illustrates the analytic we developed within our research and takes the reader through it concept by concept, integrating it with the Market-Town research as we go along. It constitutes an invitation to think beyond existing approaches to community and community research, to work in a way that allows the investigation of our own contemporary commonality, our communal being-ness, using tools appropriate to the site of investigation. Most of all, we are working with a desire to place sociality, our 'being with others' (Bauman, 2000, p63) in public, in common, at the very centre of our investigation. We want to make this 'sociologically relevant within sociological practice' (Bauman, op cit), indeed, not just for sociology but for all social sciences. In short, we want to reverse the othering of community and communal being-ness within social scientific investigation. We propose that the progressive narrative of modernist notions of community renders it impossible to begin where we want to begin. Perhaps, we can make this clear by alluding to an image very prevalent in texts for those beginning to study psychology—the duck/rabbit image. When you look at it one way, it is a duck, and then again if you look another way, it becomes a rabbit. Which is the figure? Which, the ground? It is common to understand community as an object composed of people who live in the same place or have the same interests. But our starting point is not this; it is relational linkages. Community as a term depends upon its root, which equally exists in common, commune, communication. Community then implies a sense of holding something in common, sharing and communing with one another. It is this sense that we hold as the basis for understanding community today. Not a thing created out of people happening to share a location or interest, but a set of processes and practices, actions that are constantly moving and changing, continually creating and transforming the communal. The term we use is 'communal being-ness', the action of being in common. It is this which shows us the centrality of inter-relationality for understanding the actions and processes of community. It is this we explore, building up a vocabulary and an analytic, using it in our research as we develop the argument of the book.

The book is divided into three parts. Part I builds up the analytic. Chapter 1 investigates the background to social scientific research about community, begins to introduce our framework, and also presents to the reader our research site, the town that we call Market-Town.

Chapter 2 develops the philosophical basis for our analytic and introduces the work of Hannah Arendt. It also introduces the reader to our first examples from Market-Town.

Chapter 3 introduces Arendt's concept of the 'space of appearance', illustrating it with a discussion of the significance of a track used by people to walk from one area of the town to another. It also takes us, the reader, to a community anti-poverty programme on a council estate.

Chapter 4 introduces the concept of meaning-in-common and uses this to explore a number of examples, but most especially that of an open-air swimming pool that closed some years ago but whose meanings and memories unite large sections of the townspeople.

Part II develops our analytic, weaving together concepts and fieldwork examples from the town to show how this approach can be used.

Chapter 5 develops the analytic further by bringing in the concept of the 'web of relations'. The chapter also allows us to understand the centrality of a particular hotel as a meeting point for the wealthy inhabitants of the county in which Market-Town sits.

In Chapter 6, we meet Henry St, a location in the centre of Market-Town. We encounter it mostly in the recollections of residents before most of the buildings were torn down as part of post-war 'slum clearance' and the inhabitants moved to a newly built council estate. In the chapter, the communal being-ness of this place and moment is contrasted with the present of Market-Town.

The third part of the book offers analyses of two aspects of community currently addressed in social policy: volunteering in Chapter 7 and community policing in Chapter 8. Chapter 9 concludes the book by exploring the implications of the approach developed within the book for the future of community research.

Part I

Setting Out the Analytic

1

Building the Analytic

'Community' is a word pervasive within all manner of media and daily conversation, just as it is in the academy. With its discursive presence and its emotional power, it has a major presence in agendas of governments and policy makers and beyond in the daily rhetoric of families, individuals and the academy.

Nor is this a surprise, for as Graham Crow notes (2002), 'community' stands as a convenient shorthand term for the broad realm of local social arrangements beyond the private sphere of home and family, but more familiar to us than the impersonal institutions of the wider 'society'. As such, community is a word with manifold meanings, uses and conceptualisations: an elastic word serving multiple agendas.

Community is a word routinely described both as confused and, equally routinely, by many academics at least, as 'theoretically worthless'. Fraser (1989, p. 60) observes, "community" is a tricky concept, ambiguous, incapable of agreement, permeated with value judgements, contradictorily, emotionally powerful yet somehow incapable of social science encapsulation'. While Anthony Cohen (1985, p. 11) rather tetchily announces, in terms all social scientists would recognise—'community

© The Author(s) 2016
D. Studdert, V. Walkerdine, *Rethinking Community Research*,
DOI 10.1057/978-1-137-51453-0_1

is one of those words—like "culture", "myth", "ritual", "symbol"—bandied around in ordinary, everyday speech, apparently readily intelligible to speaker and listener, which when imported into the discourse of social science causes immense problems.' There are many other academics of the same opinion: Taylor (1987), Mandelbaum (2000), Mason (2000), Keller (2003).

This antipathy attached to the concept was indeed one minor motivating factor in our decision to examine what it was about the word which drew such aversion. It led us to explore why such a concept, one which superficially at least should have been central to any science of the social, might simultaneously be so disliked and ignored.

The first thing that became apparent from our examination, was that these responses were those of the academy, not of the general public nor, indeed, of government—something which confirms Cohen's observation. Furthermore, commentators and sociologists overcome the discrepancy between the account of the academic uselessness of the term and the public view of community, by labelling the latter 'emotional'. It is claimed that the popularity of the term is simply an outcome of the emotional investment placed in it by the public (Bauman 2001a)—a lingering and sentimental attachment to the term and the emotions it evokes. It is a feel-good word, an emotional response, a 'spray-on term' (Rose 1999).

When academics speak in these terms the insinuation is that emotional equals irrational and confused (Bauman 2001a is a good example) and, further, that this irrational/emotional public faith in the term is ultimately the cause and source of the ongoing confusion. However, when we began our investigation, we discovered that this confusion is almost exclusively an academic concern and that it revolves around the misfit between academic configurations of what community is, set against the popular notion.

It was with this in mind that we began to develop, through two specific interventions, a book (Studdert 2006) and a report (Walkerdine and Studdert 2011), a critique of the failure of social sciences to satisfactorily investigate and conceptualise the topic.

As we did so, we began to see that this ambivalence towards the term, far from being particular to the late twentieth century, had in fact been present historically within the social sciences since their inception, a statement particularly pertinent for Sociology itself. It also became clear that this 'othering' of community was present in the work of Comte, the father of Sociology and, further, that the accompanying theoretical denuding of the concept and the ongoing responses of hope and disdain which had accompanied it throughout the discipline's history, all had their source in the very terms in which the veracity of the discipline as a discipline had been established.

The central contention of both the report and the book was that the academic investigation of community was currently gridlocked, primarily because conceptual tools and modes of thinking about it were inadequate to the task. Further, despite changes of terminology, these almost always represented, as we will go on to demonstrate, new labels on old bottles and that, as such, the terms and mode of thinking about community, at least as academic topic, had remained fundamentally the same throughout the history of the discipline.

This made us quite optimistic about the possibilities afforded by our research for a re-thinking of community. Yet something strange seemed to occur when we discussed our critique with fellow academics. The usual response was a disdainful, 'we know' 'we know'. It rang through many conversations, yet we found no evidence of this claimed prior understanding in texts, nor indeed did there appear to be any serious engagement with the issues we hoped to raise. Between 2002 and 2015, there were a grand total of two books published in British Sociology relating directly to thinking about community as a term (Delanty 2002; Studdert 2006). The term was constantly used in notions of 'community health', 'community policing' and 'community education', but almost without exception, the dedicated chapters in these books concerning the topic were mind-numbingly similar, little more than expositions of what the same books openly described as a term lacking in conceptual usefulness.

Confronting these responses, we came to understand that there were four conflated reasons why the social sciences, as a general field, baulked at engagement with the topic of community or the issues it raised. These were as follows:

1. The theoretical apparatus through which social sciences investigates and discusses community is simply insufficient or incapable of con-

ceptualising the topic in a sophisticated or in-depth form (Studdert 2006). 'Social Science thinking about community, was often little more than a series of descriptors'—location, interest, (Aull Davies and Jones 2003, p. 5). Superficial and reductionist, these bare descriptors function as much to curtail investigation of community, as they do to provoke it. They are simply unsuitable for the task. Crucially, while this fact was recognised, the re-configuring of the existing mode of thinking about community brought into question fundamental tenets of the discipline itself, as we will demonstrate.

2. Academics of course exist in the world outside of the academy, and in that world not only are notions of community powerful, but community is a term that still is of vital interest to funding bodies and governments. This is a dilemma largely responsible for the situation in which, as Charlotte Aull Davis and Stephanie Jones (ibid) note, the continued presence of the term within the academy itself is maintained not by academic interest, but rather by a recognition 'that it is an idea with empirical meanings for our informants and one which is useful for policy makers'. Thus, in this very post-modern formulation, community is of interest not as a theoretical concept, but rather because of its usage in the popular imagination and its status among government and funding bodies.

3. Coupled with the two issues mentioned above is the general disinterest among academics, over the last 30 years, in actually studying communal being-ness in a micro sense. The reasons for this will be examined in due course. What is important to acknowledge here, is the veracity of Gordon Hughes' claim (Hughes 2007) that the investigation of the social at a micro level is regarded within the social sciences as a modernist quirk.

4. Finally, on a simple level, academics themselves contribute to this confusion by routinely continuing to use the term throughout their texts, even though, in the same text, they equally routinely say that the term lacks clarity and theoretical value. Thus, the term serves an immediate need even while it was concurrently being stripped of meaning.

These four reasons taken together account for the confusion surrounding the term and establish this is an academic problem, not a public one.

Nor, as was mentioned earlier, is this current gridlock and this attitude of ambiguity towards the term community a new thing. Indeed, it is one which has bedevilled the discipline since its inception. To fully understand why requires a brief discussion of the history of the sociology itself.

The Theoretical Deadlock Regarding the Notion of Community

By the mid to late nineteenth century, the industrialisation and state-building process known as modernity, with its resultant social displacements and its worldwide destruction of rural communities, was in full swing, bringing in its wake a developing need to theorise and justify the process. It was in this context that Sociology developed—hesitantly it must be said—as a discipline attuned to the calculation and measurement of society: a society, it should be noted, already positioned as co-terminious with the state.

From the very first, therefore, Sociology was positioned to explain and rationalise what contemporaries referred to as 'the social question'. Its role has been described by some as akin to 'the ideology of modernism' (Bauman 2001b).

In relation to community, the need for rationalisation and justification stemmed from the act of industrialisation itself, precisely because—beginning with the enclosure movement in Britain—the entire process was constructed out of the destruction of existing communities and existing communal traditions (Bauman 2001, p. 35).

Community, with its 'medieval' linkages of clan, religion, guild and location thus constituted precisely the target of modernisation and therefore the target of the discipline whose task was to justify the terms of modernisation. From the very first, therefore, the relation of the discipline to the notion of community was shot through with problematising ambiguities precisely because community represented the things modernism sort to overcome.

Crucially, as one reads sociologists like Comte, Marx and Durkheim, one is immediately struck by the absolute consensus regarding the destruction of these communities. Uniformly across the political spectrum, from 'radicals' like Marx to 'conservatives' like Comte, we find identical descriptions concerning this process. There never seems to be a doubt that this process is both necessary and irreversible. No one, even the champion of the proletariat, is prepared to contest the necessity for the wholesale destruction of long-standing communities.

Indeed, the only issue uniting Marx and Liberalism (apart from their underlying humanism) is their conjoint notion that these communities are bastions of superstition and barriers to progress. Naturally, justifications vary: Marx sees them as barriers to the historical mission of a conscious working class and Liberalism views them as obstacles to the march of progress, rationality, and the free individual, yet the conclusions are the same.

In hindsight, the similarities between them are probably more striking than their differences. Both are fuelled by an almost blind faith in progress; all accounts are underwritten by the primacy ascribed to abstraction, mechanistic theory and process. All call on sociality and community to adjust to the objective world out there, an adjustment of course, validated by the abstraction of hidden laws.

Indeed, it is beneath the banner of these hidden laws that the 'disembedding of the traditional order' (Beck 1998, p. 24) is inaugurated, a process begun with the French revolution and continued by the industrial revolution itself. The world that emerges from this upheaval, however, is always an incomplete one, for the terms of capitalism mean it can never be closed or finalised. It remains a slave to its own progressivist rhetoric and the political necessity to provide increasing wealth, and it always 'pushes beyond itself, it has lost order' (Freyer 1930, p. 165 quoted in Beck ibid) and can never find a new order to replace it.

Thus, for sociology as the inheritor of this discourse, the present can never attain a settled closure; it is always precarious, always in a state of crisis and revolution. Within this paradigm 'community' comes to represent, therefore, not the sociality of human-being-ness, but an historical abstraction, a 'lost paradise', a sentimental arch stone of modernism's incomplete description of itself, the ultimate, and discursive other to the ephemeral, chaotic and unfinalisable present.

No one exemplifies this more literally than Comte: his search for a positive social logic, the dual status of his work as both political project and social investigation, his preoccupation with the 'laws' of social dynamics and social stability, the primacy he places on social harmony, cohesion and concord, his biological metaphors and his commonplace Hobbesian notion that without these laws society is simply the chaotic clash of opposing interests.

And while he displays all the classic responses—responses that still inform sociology over a century later—Comte is also father to the pervasive notion of what Andrew Wernick (2000) terms the socio-theology of *l'Humanite*. That is, the abstract creation of a theoretical social simulacrum: society, in which society was understood as having the properties of a living being *over and above* individual actions of sociality, governed by abstraction/laws which it is the task of empirical investigation to establish(ibid, p. 59). In other words, Wernick is accusing Comte of attempting to model sociology on the physical sciences with its provable laws. In doing so, Comte and, by implication, sociologists following him have abandoned the detailed engagement with sensuous human life for the abstracted study of social laws.

That this ontologising of the social is conceived intellectually, (ibid, p. 60), only conceals the fact that as so conceived by Comte, this social has no centre—no 'we' as Wernick notes (ibid). Thus, it represents at its contradictory core, not so much a theory of the social, but 'a theory of the impossibility of the social' (ibid, p. 61). In short, it is a theory of the social without human sociality.

This template, this construction of the social without sociality in which commonality is subsumed beneath abstraction, remains an ongoing feature of many attempts to model social being-ness. 'Networks', for instance, and network analysis are precisely such a 'theory of the social without human sociality' (Donati and Archer 2012) and an abstract social simulacrum in that sense.

What are notions of 'a new civic space' (Keane 1998, p. 19) or the 'coming community' (Agamben 1993) or notions of capital rich and capital poor, but re-runs of Comte's initial re-casting of lived community as society abstract sequels.

When Lefebvre (1991) or Keller (1984) recast the social as everyday life and in the process omit certain elements based upon a prior abstraction (Lefebvre op cit, p. 133; Keller op cit, p. 15), a higher order, what are they doing but repeating Comte's original moment of exclusion?

When Wernick (op cit) states that there is no social present in Comte's society and therefore his political project is also 'out of kilter' because it seeks to define human-being-ness in a way which theoretically it implicitly denies (ibid, p. 62), is this not a criticism equally applicable to all these accounts of community?

Almost all these issues originate in the work of Tonnies (2001), an account foundational to what is optimistically termed: the sociological approach to community. Tonnies' work is indeed so well known and so often described, there is no need to rehearse his entire argument here (Studdert 2006, p. 21ff; Delanty 2002).

What needs mentioning here however, primarily because it is so rarely touched upon, are the problems inherent within his account and the manner in which accounts, modern and post-modern, constantly repeat these unresolved problems like someone hitting their head violently on a brick wall.

Let us begin with the simplistic dichotomy of two ideal pure states: Gemeinschaft and Gesellschaft.[1] This mode of thinking, where social

---

[1] Gesellschaft (often translated as society).

For Tonnies, family life is the general basis of life in the Gemeinschaft and as such the form finds its most perfect expression in village and town life. Indeed, the village community and the town themselves can be considered as large families, the various clans and houses representing the elementary organisms of its body: guilds, corporations and offices, the tissues and organs of the town. Here, original kinship and inherited status remain an essential, or at least the most important, condition of participating fully in common property and other rights.

Conversely, the city is typical of Gesellschaft in general. It is essentially a commercial town and, insofar as commerce dominates its productive labour, a factory town. Its wealth is capital: wealth which, in the form of trade, usury or industrial capital, is used and multiplies. Capital is the means for the appropriation of products of labour or for the exploitation of workers. The city is also the centre of science and culture, hand in hand with commerce and industry. Here, for instance, the arts must make a living; they are exploited in a capitalistic way as is every activity and so, spurred by commerce, thought, in all its forms, spreads and changes with astonishing rapidity. Speeches and books through mass distribution become stimuli of far-reaching importance while the arts themselves become commodified and exploited.

being-ness is constantly described in sharp and mutually exclusive con-figurations of two entirely distinct and ideal states (what sociology likes to term a 'type'), is perhaps the most obvious and pervasive of these influences and continues to configure accounts of the social to this day: Cassell (1993), for instance, distinguishes between the cosmopolitan of elites and the tribalism of local communities; the latter of course being insular and parochial; Putnam (1990, 2001) has his 'broken' commu-nities and his social capital-rich communities characterised in precisely the same manner. Giddens has his traditional communities and his new communities of choice (Giddens 1998, p. 37). Communitarians have their disappearing communities which they seek to resurrect, defined by traditional virtues: thrift and hard work, and their modern communities defined by, guess what, their opposite: individualism, self-interest and perspectives (Sandel 1996, pp. 84–85). When Fukuyana (1995, p. 27) and Giddens (1998 p 86)' state an opposition to 'embedded communi-ties of place'—whose work are they repeating?

Anderson is another from this school of dichotomous touch-ups with his imagined community and his traditional community (Anderson 1991). Sociological Foucauldians (Rose 1999) Young (1999) have their non-existent community and the community arising as a form of gov-ernance.[2] The list is exhaustive and exhausting. Cohen (1985) inaugu-rates the notion of the modern community of interest, a community detached from location, configured of course in contrast to the one grounded in location: a re-configuration straight out of Gemeinschaft and Gesellschaft.

Indeed, it is fair to say that this simplistic dichotomy, where one pure form replaces another, has underwritten sociology's attitude to com-munity ever since Tonnies (Bauman 2001, op cit). Furthermore these replacements have no more lived experience within them than Comte's.

---

[2] We would claim that this traditional duality arises in a slightly altered form within Sociological Foucauldian work, primarily because unlike Foucault himself, they conflate discourse and practice. Thus, according to Rose (1999) community does not exist, however in the name of community, the public is endorsing and participating in forms of governance, for example, reading schemes and so on. If the public are participating in such schemes in the name of community, then clearly this is a community created by something termed governance and further if the public are responding to community and participating in this idea that it is community, then they are participating in. Oh the wicked webs we weave when we try to make discourse and practice correspond.

Tonnies' work bequeaths other legacies as well—historical discontinuity being one. This is the notion that community is a historically specific social formation belonging to a particular time and a particular place, something reproduced in varied terminology in Bauman (2001), Giddens (1997) and Agamben 1993)—a formulation which allows sociologists to claim that what is taking place in the contemporary world, what surrounds them in their own life, is not and never can be, 'community'. A subtle displacement which means—as we shall see—that the only language possible for contemporary social formations is the language of the state. What they do not say is that the particular form that community takes in any historical period is specific and that we need to be able to engage with that form in its specificity, the position taken in this volume.

There are other important legacies as well: one being the construction of two personality types, each normative within his foundational dichotomy. For, while Tonnies portrays the Gesellschaft city as dehumanising and implicitly decries the loss of spiritual and creative unity which he claims had personified the Gemeinschaft, the destruction of Gemeinschaft (notice he speaks of it in the singular) is attributed, not to greed and capitalism, but rather to a 'natural' outcome of expansive personality, an invisible process against which opposition is futile and to which, of course, human beings and the social must adjust. This recourse to psychology to explain events neatly naturalises and de-politicises the particularities of dispossession, while disappearing the actions of human beings and their responsibility for these actions into the rarefied abstractions of history and process. In this configuration, the role of the rational unitary individual (Henriques et al. 1984) is stressed both as an agent for causation (as a bearer of the new emerging social forms) and as the outcome of the development of the Gesellschaft, a formulation which, in its circularity, boldly anticipates a century of such sophistic circularity within Sociology. Once again, this remains a staple of interventions into thinking about community. For instance, when Giddens (1997) enunciates reflexivity as characteristic of social forms emerging from the breakdown of traditional communities what is he doing but postulating the same notions inherent within Tonnies? Indeed, Giddens' mimicry extends to the question whether such 'reflexivity' functions as cause or effect. Finally, in exactly the same manner as his model Tonnies, Giddens postulates it as both simultaneously (Outhwaite 1998, p. 26; Studdert

2006, p. 28). Similarly, the 'institutionalized individualism' of Ulrich Beck (Beck and Beck-Gercheim 2002), with its *homo inconstantus*, its subject freed from traditionalism's 'zombie categories' of class and gender, now enmeshed in a plethora of bureaucratic regulations yet somehow free to embrace their self-reinvention, change their identities and rewrite their biographies according to current whim, is another position that also duplicates Tonnies' original foundation.

The relation and resort of Sociology to psychology is an old one, with Sociology often both critiquing psychology and yet constantly turning to some underpinning psychology as a support when it suits (Blackman and Walkerdine 2001).

At this point we trust that enough has been said[3] to sustain our claim that investigation of community and the relation of the human being to forms of social formation is 'grid-locked'. Indeed, even this brief examination demonstrates how the complex conceptual history of the social sciences constrains the possibility of an alternative investigation of contemporary community.

This sketch demonstrates that the problem with the concept of community for the social sciences runs deep within the disciplinary history of Sociology. Our analytic begins, therefore, from the starting point that far from it being the case that relational linkages have disappeared, and that the state/individual or market/individual axis now has pre-eminence, it may well be the case that the inter-relationality that creates the possibility of communal being is alive and well. The social sciences, constrained by their history, simply lack the means to investigate it.

This means that if we are to seek a way to investigate the presence of communal meanings and linkages, we have to move entirely outside these failed forms of thinking and theorizing community.

Overcoming Obstacles

The next step in our process is to examine the two main obstacles confronting any attempt to conceptualise community within existing accounts. These two obstacles are implicated in all accounts mentioned

---

[3] For further examples, please refer to Studdert (2006).

to this point and in many others besides (Studdert 2006, op cit; Chapters 5 and 6). They stem both from the discipline's self-anointed role as the 'ideology of modernism' (Bauman, op cit) and from the ingrained and common place use of the mechanistic method. The first being the means for social and political recognition of the discipline's worth and the second stemming from the discipline's desire for 'scientific' validation.

It is our claim that these two elements, operating simultaneously, are the key arches of the gridlock concerning investigation of why 'things are so and not otherwise' (Weber 1949) and that only through the overcoming of these roadblocks can progress be made in the task of facilitating investigation of communal being-ness.

The State/Individual Axis

It has become apparent throughout this discussion about the topic of communing 'that modernist social scientific conceptualisation situates community within a pre-given but unacknowledged framework' (Bauman 2001, p. 35). This is a framework that, from the outset, constrains the capacity of the discipline to explain, or even adequately engage, with the topic of community. Primarily the demand is for these accounts to conform to a model, both of what Sociology is and what social science investigation amounts to.

In particular, it was argued 'that the weak conceptualisation of community within these accounts is a direct outcome of their articulation of community as subservient to the defining modernist axis of liberal individual and liberal state, and that, in varied ways, this conceptual subservience is reductive of the theoretical space rightly belonging to community' (Studdert 2006, op cit). Thus, community and the state are discursively produced within this paradigm as objects of knowledge based upon a series of truth claims articulated in a double movement by which an ideologically constructed state and individual are defined as natural, while the principle that generates the overall configuration remains concealed (Lefort 1986, p. 11).

Within such a subservient theoretical landscape, the Tonnies' derived notions of community are incapable of adequately explaining the historical sedimentation of social institutions, the manifestations of sociality in action or the social construction of subjectivity. It is precisely for this reason that Dumont (1986) describes Western accounts of social being-ness as superficial.

Academic subservience and the privileging of the state/individual axis take varied forms and even in accounts specifically pointing towards inter-relationality and socially derived subjectivity, concern for the social tends to be backgrounded and not actually under-stood as existing within specific times and places (e.g. Gergen 1994; Walkerdine, date (ESRC lecture)). In short, most of the work con-cerning inter-relationality is loath to step beyond this modernist privileging. This theoretical subservience exists as a direct outcome of modernity's assertion that value in a sphere depends exclusively upon how well subjects measure up to the norms 'proper' to that sphere (Lash 1989, p. 9).

For our part, we argue that the primacy allocated to the state/indi-vidual axis is maintained in texts with a series of moves common to all texts relating to community. These are as follows:

1. *The naturalisation of the individual within social theory*
   Community within modernity is, and continues to be, proposed as an instrumental means for individual self-realisation. The individual emerges from its own efforts and subjectivity is contained and sourced (somehow) within the individual. Such individual rationality is under-stood as the outcome of a naturalised developmental sequence inher-ently above and prior to sociality itself, for example, Darwin (1859) and Piaget (1950). This privileging, confirms the derivative role ascribed to community as a source of social subjectivity and it posi-tions sociality and community as simply stages for the unfolding and enacting of rationality, not its source.
   Despite the discrediting of the more simplistic aspects of the fully formed rational individual, many texts about community retain this totem in a coded and euphemistic form (Young 1999 is one example). Commentators have simply often by-passed this theoretical discredit-ing by resorting to alternative terms, such as, ability (Giddens 1999),

through the foundational use of individualistic psychology or by the utilisation of terms such as 'community of interest' which represent this notion in a concealed form.[4]

2. *The naturalisation of the state within social theory*
From the state side of the state/individual axis, community within theoretical social science has always been, and continues to be, implicitly theorised as an *effect* of the state.

This distorted ordering is maintained within the social sciences by a series of characteristic, conceptual substitutions for the term community, frequently without any historical analysis of the different developments of each concept. Terms such as 'network society', 'everyday life', 'new space', 'civil society', 'trust', 'social capital' and 'network theory'—continually produce a disempowered, isolated and context-free, social world while implicitly reconfirming the validity of the state as the necessary arbitrator: the impartial, natural and most elevated form for the organisation of sociality. Within such a 'truth-regime', these conceptual substitutions utilised by the social sciences remain inadequate to conceptualise a self-sufficient description of communal human being-ness as a valued series of actions *unto themselves*. Thus, they remain unable to provide a full account of social being-ness and social inter-relationality. In relation to community, all texts examined over a prolonged period contain multiple examples and versions of this approach (Chapter 5 in Studdert 2006 discusses variations and modes of this approach across a wide gamut of work). The result is the configuration of communal meanings as irrelevant, not worthy of investigation and community itself as a supine form, one in which the state and the individual provide all the motivational, creative and actionable elements.

---

[4] Moreover notions of fluidity claiming to solve this issue do so only by collapsing agency and structure into a soup with one flavour (Donati and Archer Margaret 2012). We would claim that a true account of socially derived being-ness has no need for a normative approach but rather is capable of accounting for differences in particularity derived from communal being-ness in common. Something in our judgement these accounts are unwilling or unable to provide. Thus, whatever the value of these accounts in relation to other fields, in relation the investigation of communal being-ness, they remain stubbornly normative and incapable of accounting for relation of, particularity, action and communal being-ness. Thus, the individual in either method is either surreptitiously re-inserted or theoretically 'disappeared', neither situation being of much use for the investigation of community.

The state and the individual confirm each other's veracity while disqualifying other forms of social inter-relationality.

The issue for the discipline is that, despite some attempts, the discipline has been unable to find way to approach the topic beyond these limitations.[5]

The Mechanistic Structure Underlying These Accounts

Mechanistic theory is characterised by a far-reaching, pervasive fragmentation. Parts are demarcated from each other, from the whole, from the social world of human being-ness, as well as from the subjective world of human consciousness (Bohm 1980, p. 16; Arendt 1958 op cit; Latour 1993). The world is reduced—through a process of 'discovery', which in reality is just as much a process of construction—to a set of basic elements which function externally to each other, interact mechanically, are separated in space and are each inscribed with an essentialist nature, entirely distinct from either the whole or any other fundamental units (Bohm 1985, p. 3). Elements are constituted as parts of an impersonal and universal machine: society, the basic order of which is constructed from the impersonal, machine-like, interaction of these nominated, demarcated and independent parts.

Thinking in a mechanistic manner permeates every aspect of our lives. One example is the relation of the state to its citizens. The 'state' is precisely conceived as just such an impersonal machine and, in liberal political theory at least, is composed of millions of free citizens all essentialised as supposedly rational, all fragmented into their individuality, denied (at least theoretically) other forms of inter-relationship and who, by their individual voting, construct and maintain the state as the outcome of their supposed intentions. The commonly held neo-liberal picture of the market is another obvious practical example.

The more one delves into the 400-year history of modernity, the more one is constantly confronted by modernity as a process of fragmentation,

---

[5] See note 2.

separation and, finally, re-unification through representation and symbolisation (Latour 1992, op cit).

That is a chain in which 'every assemblage of things is transformed into a mere multitude, a society in which, just like mathematics, each individual is defined in the likeness of others, but cannot see it' (Lefort 1986, op cit, p. 167), and in which social being-ness possesses 'the same validity and no more significance than the mathematical curve' (Arendt 1958, op cit, p. 267). A mechanistic view of the communal splinters community and lived experience into separated actions; actions taking place in nominated and separated spheres. Within these spheres, all actions follow a similar normative course. Thus, this model denies both the inter-relationality of life and the capacity of human being-ness for particular actions and being-ness-in-common across demarcated spheres. Trying to investigate community inter-relationally within this model thus becomes impossible, because human beings and the action of human beings can never be seen in its wholeness.

Of course, mechanistic theory, as Latour observes (1993, op cit), is a close blood relative of Hobbesian and Cartesian thought. Indeed, it reproduces the primordial Cartesian separation of personal subjectivity from the wider world, and makes the latter accessible only through hidden laws to which we have no access via our senses. This Cartesian split provides the basis for the mechanistic elevation of process (Arendt 1958, op cit, p. 105, p. 232) just as the Hobbesian counterpart provides the reasoning behind both the mechanical metaphors and the elevation of conflict over co-operation. Thus mechanistic thinking (Studdert 2006, Chapter 6, op cit) relegates communal being-ness and, indeed, action itself (Arendt 1958, pp. 230–236) to a subsidiary role as simply the expression of these hidden laws and the abstract thought that drives them.

Both these elements, the state/individual axis and the primacy accorded mechanistic theory, represent impassable barriers in the task of describing sociality and communal being-ness as actions unto themselves. At the most fundamental they block investigation of communal being-ness and communal action by the attaching of pre-emptive abstractions which foreclose the possibility of investigation itself.

We argue that the progressivist and modernist narrative of community renders impossible the investigation of the qualities central to communal being-ness. These are hybridity, plurality, inter-relationality and action.

Hybridity: all the social being-ness we engage in on an everyday basis contains other forms of communal being-ness. We bring communal meanings derived from social being-ness into different social arenas constantly: work sociality into time with friends, online into off-line and so forth. Without acknowledging hybridity, we cannot think about inter-relationality.

Plurality: we all belong to various communal formations, of various sizes and degrees of involvement and investment. Within each 'community', there is a plurality of perspectives: yet the validity of these multiple perspectives and their role and place in communal being-ness is utterly lost when they are subsumed under single explanations of location or interest (Dumont 1986, op cit; Dussel 1998; Nancy 1991).

Action: the Western philosophical tradition privileges thought over action (see Studdert 2006, Chapter 1 for a historical analysis). The issue for the process of analysing community is that community is the action of 'being with', not solitary contemplation.

Inter-relationality: community is also inter-relational. Linkage exists both in the sense of communal meaning and in the sense of physical linkage between and within communities. The capacity to investigate inter-relationality is crucial to the understanding of communal being-ness.

Having explained this at some length, we trust that it is now clear how social scientific investigation of community has reached an impasse.

This book therefore presents an alternative analytic for the investigation of communal being-ness in all its lived experience. To this end we are not inventing a theory of community, defined as a something which explains what community *is*, which privileges some element as the key to understanding *all* human social activity. Rather, we are developing an analytic specific to social activity, which is aimed at valuing social activity as an action in itself, an action of sociality without pre-emptive closure or essentialist form and investigating it accordingly. However, we do not propose that sociality is a pure action, quite the reverse as our account will make clear (Chapter 2).

The approach attempts to find a way to analyse and express hybridity, action, inter-relationality and plurality. We are seeking an inter-relational *analytic* which allows us to investigate sociality as a combined manifestation of the particular and the common as a practice *in itself.*

Crucially, this analytic is not a re-privileging of any element. As Arendt states clearly in terms we entirely endorse:

> Academic philosophy… has been dominated by the never ending reversals of idealism and materialism, of transcendentalism and immanentism, of realism and nominalism, of hedonism and asceticism and so on. What matters here is the reversibility of all these systems, that they can be "turned "upside down" or "downside up" without requiring for such reversals either historical events or changes in the structural elements involved. …It is still the same tradition the same intellectual game with paired antitheses that rules, to an extent, the famous modern reversals of spiritual hierarchies, such as Marx's turning Hegelian dialectic upside down, or Nietzsche's revaluation of the sensual and natural as against the supernatural (Arendt 1958, p. 293).

This is the means through which Arendt steps philosophically outside the Hegelian tradition so prominent in, and constrictive of, Western thought. Using this analytic, we do not present community is either an unproblematic good or an unproblematic bad. Indeed, we hold no value attitude to it at all. Nor do we think community is any one thing. In this sense, we do not need a view of what community *is,* precisely because we prefer to analyse *how it works.*

The analytic to be developed here is one that proposes all actions of sociality as involved in the construction of the particular and temporary social being-ness in common. It therefore does not seek pure forms or Weberian types, nor does it value one form of sociality over another. Further, it proposes that all social formations are composed, created and maintained through the actions of sociality in common. It sets itself against notions of macro and micro and does not propose itself as an ontology of either a hierarchical or a flat sort.[6]

---

[6] Given that DeLanda (2004, p. 58) describes an hierarchical ontology as 'based on relations between general types and particular instances is hierarchical', with 'each level representing a differ-

We simply want to see 'communing' and the terms under which it is actioned as what it is: for me and you, for him and her, for them and us, a multiple activity, a being-in common, a being-ness which happens (Nancy op cit, p. 149) an inter-relational, ongoing multiplicity of socialites

What we propose is that an academic re-thinking of our contemporary communal being-ness is overdue. That the communal world which exists and sustains us has been 'disappeared' from our imagination; that we have lost the capacity to even think its loss. That too many assertions and fantasies like the 'disappearance of community' or 'future communities' or community as synonymous with the state or reductive notions of networks, micro-circuits, and so on have allowed us to avoid the investigation of our own concrete and contemporary communal existence. That this commonality of ours has been absent for too long from the accounts of the social we give ourselves.

This monograph is offered in the hope that together we can break out of the current academic and social gridlock concerning communal being-ness and once again think about this social being-ness of ours: what it consists of, and requires; what supports it and what undermines it.

Finally, as an analytic, the work is offered in the hope that it can re-establish the linkage between evidential investigation and analysis. We have therefore chosen to centre this monograph round a series of questions relating to aspects of Market-Town's communal being-ness. Thus every chapter has a combination of theory, data and discussion which, taken in their totality, can hopefully present new possibilities for community research, new applied methods, and new philosophical perspectives on wider issues relating to our social being-ness.

We have chosen to preserve the anonymity of this town, partially because it allows us to engage with all aspects of town life without unfairly opening the town residents to scrutiny.

---

ent ontological category (organism, species, genera) our approach for reasons to be outline in the course of the monograph clearly is not of such an order'.

Conversely, given his defining of a flat ontology as made 'exclusively of unique, singular individuals, differing in spatio-temporal scale but not in ontological status (DeLanda 2004, p. 58) it is also clear, as our text will make plain, that the proposed analytic is not that order either'.

Market-Town

Located in a scenic, largely agricultural landscape, in a relatively wealthy, southern county of Britain, Market-Town, in 2012, had a population of approximately 14,200 inhabitants.

It is a picturesque location surrounded by mountains and hills and traversed by two rivers. In common with many towns in this region it has a castle and various remnants of medieval fortification which still exist in parts of the town.

The town has long made its living, serving conjointly the surrounding farming communities and a number of ex-industrial communities located within a close radius. Unlike many of these latter communities, however, Market-Town has a strong cross section of incomes and classes. The main street typifies this, being a collection of second-hand shops and upmarket boutiques. There are a number of hotels ranging from one which has a ballroom and five bars where the well-heeled gather for the famous scone and cream afternoon tea, to ones of the more sawdust and broken teeth variety. The middle class and commuter belt house owners live in the centre and south of the town, while a working-class estate sits on a windy hill circling the town's northern edge.

The town is home to a significant number of older people, with 32 % of the local population aged over 60, according to the 2011 census. In this, it reflects trends across the wider county which has, over recent decades, become a prime retirement site for people from all over the country. Ethnically it is a largely white town with pockets of overseas Asian nurses recruited to work in the local hospital. It is also clear from our data and interviews that many people in the town have relatives and extended familial relationships within the town itself.

There is a single comprehensive school and ten primary schools in the town and immediate environs.

The town has a long history on its present site. Beginning in the nineteenth century, growth was steady, related in large part to the effects of the industrial revolution, resulting in a considerable industrial presence. Remnants of the industrial revolution dot the surrounding countryside: canals and railway bridges in particular. The development of the local agricultural economy also contributed to the growth and regional importance of the town. The town has had a general market building for over 400 years and a livestock market for approximately the same period. There were once woollen mills close to what is now the centre of the town and the 1900s saw accelerated development of the tanning industry, boot/shoe-making, glove-making and other leather trades. Tailors and dressmakers, hat-making, candle-making, printing, milling, iron foundries, breweries have all come and gone over the last 150 years.

The town population rose from over 2000 in 1801 to over 5000 by 1851 and nearly 8000 by 1901. Since 1945, however, the town has grown dramatically, though currently geographical factors severely constrain future housing. Prior to the 1980s, there were a large number of local employers whose factories produced a range of industrial products, but the last of these closed in the decade that followed. Currently, the main employer is the local hospital and service industries in general. Several interviewees told us that wages in the town were the lowest in the county though this could not be independently confirmed.

The town has a wide variety of churches, including traditional denominations and recent charismatic healing assemblies. Crime is very low in the town, principally, according to figures provided by the local police, consisting of various forms of Anti-Social Behaviour Orders, some burglaries and domestic violence. It is important to note, however, that while the town is relatively wealthy, the estate sits very high in various national multiple deprivation indices. A fact often 'lost' in the overall figures of the much richer county.

There are many volunteer and sporting associations in the town ranging from outdoor activities to historical societies and town preservation and action committees. There are tennis, cricket, rugby and football clubs as well as other sporting groups of a less competitive nature: kayaking and so forth. The most active of the volunteer groups, at least in relation to the life of the town, is the Market-Town Civic Society which meets monthly in the upmarket hotel mentioned previously. There is a local theatre which puts on plays and concerts by visiting artists as well as various interest groups, history societies, masons, boy scouts and guides, and so on. The town is administrated by a town council which has little real power and is dominated by small business interests and the county council. Approximately 80 % of the town councillors are also simultaneously serving county councillors.

Until the late 1950s, extended working-class families had resided for 400 years in streets located in the middle of the town, principally centred on Henry Street. The area was distinguished by its medieval housing, typified by large houses which ran around and opened onto internal courtyards. It lacked sewage or running water. As recorded by one interviewee this area was a 'no go' area self-policed by its working inhabitants.

In the late 1950s, the government without consultation began relocating people from Henry Street to the outskirts of the town and onto the new estate on the periphery of the town. This was termed in the jargon of the time 'slum clearance'.

The town population has a very developed sense of itself as a 'special place' with a 'special feeling' which, as one respondent put it, 'punches above its weight' in regard to energy within the town and communal spirit and feeling about the town.

In the next chapter, we will begin the development of the analytic, by discussing the terms for the construction of social being-ness.

Bibliography

Agamben, G. (1993). *The coming community*. Minneapolis: University of Minneapolis Press.

Arendt, H. (1958). *The human condition*. Chicago: University of Chicago Press.

Aull Davies, C., & Jones, S. (2003). *Welsh communities: New ethnographic perspectives*. Cardiff: University of Wales Press.

Beck, U. (1998). *Democracy without enemies*. Cambridge: Polity.

Beck, U., & Beck-Gercheim, E. (2002). *Individualisation: Institutional individualism and it political and social consequences*. London: Sage.

Blackman, L., & Walkerdine, V. (2001). *Mass hysteria: Critical psychology and media studies*. Basingstoke: Palgrave.

Bohm, D. (1980). *Wholeness and the implicate order*. London: Routledge.

Bohm, D. (1985). *Unfolding meaning*. London: Routledge.

Cassell, P. (Ed.). (1993). *Giddens reader*. Basingstoke: Macmillan.

Cohen, A. P. (1985). *The symbolic construction of community*. London: Tavistock Press.

Crow, G. (2002). *Social solidarities: Theories, identities and social change.* Buckinghamshire: Open University Press.

Delanty, G. (2002). *Community.* London: Routledge.

Donati, P., & Archer Margaret, S. (2012). *The relational subject.* Cambridge: Cambridge University Press.

Dumont, L. (1986). *Essays on individualism.* Chicago: University of Chicago Press.

Dussel, E. (1998). Beyond eurocentrism: The world system and the links of modernity. In Jameson, F. & M. Miyoshi (Eds.), *The cultures of globalisation.* Durham: Duke University Press.

Fraser, N. (1989). *Unruly practices.* Minneapolis: University of Minnesota Press.

Fukuyana, F. (1995). *Trust.* London: Hamish Hamilton.

Gergan, K. (1994, May). Exploring the postmodern: Perils or potentials? *American Psychologist, 49*(5), 412–416.

Giddens, A. (1998). *The third way: The renewal of social democracy.* Cambridge: Polity Press.

Giddens, A. (1999). *Runaway world: How globalisation is reshaping our lives.* London: Profile.

Henriques, J., Holloway, W., Urwin, C., Venn, C., & Walkerdine, V. (1984). *Changing the subject: Psychology, social regulation & subjectivity.* London: Methuen.

Hughes, G. (2007). *The politics of crime and community.* London: Palgrave.

Keller, S. (2003). *Community.* Princeton: Princeton University Press.

Lash, S. (1989). *Sociology of post modernism.* London: Routledge.

Latour, B. (1993). *We have never been modern.* Cambridge, MA: Harvard University Press.

Lefort, C. (1986). *The political forms of modern society.* Cambridge: Polity.

Mandelbaum, S. J. (2000). *Open moral communities.* Cambridge: MIT Press.

Mason, A. (2000). *Community, solidarity and belonging.* Cambridge: Cambridge University Press.

Nancy, J.-L. (1991). *The inoperative community.* Minneapolis: University of Minnesota Press.

Outhwaite, W. (1998). Naturalism & anti-naturalism. In May, T. & M. Williams (Eds.), *Knowing the social world.* Philadelphia: Open University Press.

Piaget, J. (1950). *Explanation in sociology.* Sociological studies (pp. 30–96).

Rose, N. (1999). *Powers of freedom.* Cambridge: Cambridge University Press.

Sandel, M. J. (1996). *Democracy's discontent.* Cambridge, MA: Harvard University Press.

Studdert, D. (2006). *Conceptualising community: Beyond the state and the individual.* London: Palgrave.

Taylor, M. (1987). *The possibility of co-operation.* Cambridge: Cambridge University Press.

Tonnies, F. (2001). *Community and civil society* (edited by Harris J. and trans: Harris, J. & Hollis, M.). Cambridge: Cambridge University Press.

Walkerdine, V., & Studdert, D. (2012). *Concepts and meanings of community in the social sciences.* AHRC discussion paper for the Connected Communities Program, Swindon.

Weber, M. (1949). *On the methodology of the social sciences* (trans: Shils E.A. & Finch H.A). Glenco, IL: The Free Press.

Wernick, A. (2000). From Comte to Baudrillard: Socio-theology after the end of the social. *Theory, Culture and Society, 17*(6), 55–75.

2

How Can We Think About Social Activity?

Having taken a moment, as it were, to outline the history and contemporary situation of Market-Town, the account now thinks in general terms about sociality: what it is, why it is important and how we can begin to conceptualise it.

Given, as we have explained in Chap. 1, that the point is not to inaugurate another theory, what follows is offered as the basis for our developing analytic. This analytic is designed specifically as a social science tool for the investigation of community as a social form. Thus, the analytic is developed to fulfil its investigative task. As we discussed, classic Western academic philosophy derived from Hegel and the reactions to it, follow the path described by Arendt. That is a simple reversal of values. In this ongoing activity, one pure and therefore privileged form replaces another. So, Marx turns Hegel's idealism into materialism, for example. This is the step Arendt avoids. This avoidance is achieved because all elements in her account of the social life of human beings are linked inter-relationally.

Action, for instance, takes its particular form from the inter-relational context, the terms under which it occurs, as does every other element. This means that if we wish to understand 'community', we cannot do

© The Author(s) 2016
D. Studdert, V. Walkerdine, *Rethinking Community Research*,
DOI 10.1057/978-1-137-51453-0_2

so by understanding it as pre-given categories and pure forms, which we then seek in the social world.

The account presented in this book uses our approach to analyse the specificity of community as it is created at one time and in one place. Specificity is achieved not because the elements involved are too particular to be common, but because the terms under which communal being-ness is achieved vary. As we will demonstrate, particular outcomes are the result of particular configurations of general aspects in common. Thus other locations will share commonality with Market-Town, but the specific outcomes will vary in their detail.

For this reason, we are arguing that all instances of social analysis must operate in investigative specificity, outside of overarching abstractions. As Arendt makes clear, there is no reason to believe that any of the abstractions like 'globalisation', 'networks', 'fluidity', 'history' or 'rationality' actually exist. Therefore, what is required certainly as an initial step is to investigate social life directly, putting aside the application of prior abstractions.

In this sense, such abstractions pre-emptively define what it investigates (Sewell 2005, p. 319, also, p. 128). Like Sewell (op cit) we argue that it is better to define clearly what we are discussing and move beyond what he terms 'the peculiar vagueness', 'oversaturated(ness)' and 'polysemy' (op cit, p. 314) of the term community.

From this perspective, we will use the terms communal being-ness and the social, in the sense defined here as 'the sum of the inter-dependence of human relations' (Baker 1994).[1] The proposed analytic investigates social being-ness in this direct form 'because nothing entitles us to believe that man (*sic*) has a nature, an essence (Arendt 1958, op cit, p. 10) or a psychology, and because all of these idealisms ("products of thought") are reductive of worldly experience to thought'. 'They dull and remove us from the world from us just as they remove us from the world' (ibid, p. 321).

---

[1] It is important to grasp here that we are proposing an analytic of our shared common life. Therefore, materiality is included in the sense that it is an inter-actional element within any particular concrete example of sociality rather than as a separate determining category in its own right. We do not want to see the material and the social as two distinct entities. Rather, we want to go beyond the binary towards a notion of inter-relationality that encompasses them both.

It should also be noted that our aim accords exactly with Arendt's assertion that the first step to understanding life is to renounce the illusion of sovereignty contained within the term, 'Man'.

The first specific step we will take is to state clearly that the noun 'community' is not our preferred term. Rather, we insist that community should be considered a verb: *communing*, and *communal being-ness* as the noun; henceforth these will be the term we will use wherever possible. This is because relationality and sociality involve actions and movement, being and becoming, and are, therefore, never a static thing.

This step marks our move beyond the world of previous approaches to community which hitherto have reified it into a thing or object, a local, primordial realm of social life, a 'lower form' subject to encroachment by higher, abstract societal forces such as capitalism and the centralised state. A stage upon which these 'higher macro forms' can simply write their agendas of abstraction, as if the stage had no being-ness of its own (Nancy 1991).

So the shift to the term 'communing' reasserts not just the fundamental place of the social inter-relationality for the production of subjectivity, but also represents an open horizon, an escape from the mechanistic demarcations through which the theoretical city (Bachelard 1964) of Sociology privileges abstractions and the macro over the supposed minutiae of micro human linkages. Simultaneously, it also allows us to locate linkages and commonalities through an analytical frame. It thus avoids the intellectual philosophical game where one abstraction replaces another in a simple reversal of values. The term 'community' within a social science approach represents precisely the universalisation of a particular set of attitudes (Arendt 1958, op cit, p. 17) and this is exactly what we seek to avoid.

Thus we seek to confirm ourselves to ourselves through the presence of other people (ibid, p. 95). This slight shift in focus, rather like a split in the ice which has a narrow opening, this change of terminology goes down a long, long way.

What Is Sociality?

In approaching sociality therefore we are not aiming for a mechanistic definition, but rather a descriptive list, indicating an infinite field, incapable of ever being seen in its entirety by any one person or conceived, even by thought.

In that sense, we could understand sociality as a creating an ecological relational field (Bateson 2000), of the kind that we are beginning to understand, surround and embrace the human (e.g. biosemiotics, the microbiome, epigenetics). Thus, the field of sociality is a way of describing the totality of our inter-relations with other people, with non-humans, with buildings and materiality in its widest sense, in our life together in public, no matter how small or large, in any setting. This is the sort of interaction eternally between humans for an infinite array of particular and common reasons (Arendt, op cit, p. 46)—in short, every interaction in the public[2] world, in front of others.

It includes all actions, of which speech/utterance (Volosinov 1973) is the most important but not, however, the only or the privileged form. In short, sociality is a single field of commonality enacted in specific instances.

Every day, everywhere, sociality of different strengths and meanings is what composes our lives. It is the smile between two strangers who live in the same street, the groups chatting in the supermarket, or at work, at home, or at the school gate. It occurs when fans sing team songs at football matches. It happens in business meetings, at work, in corridors, at meetings of army officers in the mess, at steering groups large and small, voluntary or administrative. It is present in military parades or online; in projects to redeem old school buildings, to restore old houses; when groups brawl outside dance halls in ritual fighting. It occurs in the corridors of power; between journalists and politicians; when we go to the doctors or into a government building; it happens online when we intersect with web sites. It occurs constantly among

---

[2] Public in this work, as in Arendt, is used in its widest sense: in front of others; be they two, four or fourteen hundred.

the poor, the middle class and the rich. It occurs when people talk to each other or enter a twelfth-century cathedral or speak their mind about their job or give their opinions surreptitiously to each other. It is the smallest of actions, occurring infinitely in the largest of arenas and again, in the smallest. Such sociality surrounds us constantly and eternally.

Sociality is given here the widest possible actualisation: as action in common between human beings. Sociality is incalculable, porous, fluid and infinite; ultimately, unknowable as an essence, a noun or a static, idealised Weberian type. Sociality is thus something accessible only through our actions of joint and common engagement.

So we are not speaking here about a 'god place', where the totality of all relations can be seen or understood outside of our place within them. In its totality, the 'sum' of all sociality is invisible. Nonetheless this 'sum' is always present in the sense that it 'informs' and underwrites the authenticity of all other engagements. Crucially, as well, no action is more important than any other, or indeed precisely identical to any other.

The terms, 'public world', 'social world', 'common world', 'the world of our meeting place' means 'in the presence of others'. It could take place with one person or a million: indoors, outdoors or what we would commonly refer to as 'in private'.

Thus, because sociality takes place as action in this public, common world,[3] it also always contains *all* elements of worldly being-ness[4] manifested in an infinite, hybrid, ongoing, never sealed, combination of the particular, common actions comprising our lives.

---

[3] When discussing the common world, we also invoke recent debates about the Commons (Ostrom 1990), but it should be noted that the idea of the Commons presented there is far more limited than the idea of the common world presented here. That notion is an area of economic life where Commons are nominated as 'common'. Our notion of the common refers to all life in common.

[4] We are using the term being-ness here, as it implies the creation of a set of relations not co-terminious with a sense of individual identity, even if that identity is proposed as socially produced. The conceptual borders of being-ness are completely different and imply a concept in which any being is composed of a shifting set of relations that are always part of a wider web. This is not unlike the concept of assemblage within the work of Deleuze and Guattari (Marcus and Saka 2006).

Inter-relationality[5]

In 'Conceptualising Community' (2006), Studdert described Arendt's work, *The Human Condition* (1958), not as a work which simply re-privileges action over thought as some claim (D'Entreves 1994), but rather as a project dedicated to the notion of *the primacy of inter-relationality*.

Arendt's world is a social world, a common relational world where human beings are a conditioned and conditioning force, where action, freedom and identity are all limited and acted upon both by the world, and by their own location within that world. Where, if action, for instance, endows the world with meaning as Arendt claims (1958), it does so as an outcome of the fundamental conditionality of all human being-ness.

It is through this stress upon linkage, that Arendt continually asserts the primacy of lived experience, the individuality of experience, the social being of existence and crucially, the *inter-relationality* of experience (ibid, p. 321 where the two sit side by side).[6]

By posing the question 'who we are' rather than 'what we are', Arendt thus reverses the traditional Western philosophical standard which inscribes thought with prescriptive power over action (Villa 1996, op cit, p. 160) and overturns the traditional de-coupling of thought from action. Yet this reversal represents more than a simple theoretical re-privileging. Quite the contrary, even action is contained and expressed only through other interlinked conditions such as labour, work, and plurality and each of these in turn and acting together define what each of these terms 'mean'. It is this inter-relational perspective through which her picture of the social is expressed, which enunciates Arendt's work as truly radical.

---

[5] This is a truncated portion taken from Chapter 7 of *Conceptualising Community: Beyond the State and the Individual* (Studdert 2006). The manner in which Arendt shows the inter-relational aspects of labour, work and action is the primary means by which she avoids essentialising any single aspect of social existence or elevating one about the other.

[6] Of course, this type of approach, what one could call a holistic approach, is and has been commonplace since Tonnies. What we trust distinguishes our approach is that it does not begin with terms like culture, structure, culture agency, and so on, but rather begins at the very foundation of social being-ness which is the construction of social being-ness in common. And thus, it posits such being-ness in common as prior to all notions of culture structure, and so on, though, of course, they are involved in the *terms of that construction*.

Plurality, Action and Being-ness

Sociology, and the Social Sciences in general, deal precisely with action in the world; worldly action, action in public, action before others. This is also precisely the area encompassed by Hannah Arendt's notion of *vita activa* (1958) and it is through her immersion in this realm of worldly affairs that she asserts what is also the defining focus of this analytic: the primacy of being-ness, the 'who we are' (Arendt 1958, p. 10) over the metaphysical, idealised, modernist explanations of 'what we are' (ibid).[7]

Of ultimate relevance for her description of the social creation of being-ness is her location of the creation of being-ness within an inter-relational frame as an inter-relational action. This is also the key element in this analytic.

Inter-relational action for social science purposes is sociality. All elements of sociality, including speech (as distinct from discourse[8]) create what Arendt terms 'being-ness'. As such, action exists in every aspect of our lives, from the most 'mundane' to the most 'crucial'. As we shall see, inter-relational action creates being-ness in every social encounter, not just the ones to which we attach pre-emptive value. Affect or putting the washing out with friend, becomes as important for this proposed analysis as engaging with government.

As a general statement regarding the theme of 'The Human Condition', Arendt's refusal to grade actions of sociality represents a refusal to explain human commonality through the comfort of abstraction, be that abstraction psychologism (see her attack on urges (Arendt, 1958, p. 321); subjectivism (ibid, p. 284), philosophy (ibid, p. 292) or indeed any form of metaphysics (ibid, p. 262/3). She does this, just to emphasise the point, because nothing entitles us to believe that humans have a nature, an essence (ibid, p. 10) or a psychology; and because all idealisms

---

[7] It needs to be stated here clearly, that this is an approach which takes elements of Arendt's work in one particular book: *The Human Condition* (1958) and extrapolates from that an analytic specifically designed to investigate communal being-ness. It is not a critique of Arendt's overall writing or her overall approach. It uses what is useful for the tasks we have set ourselves. Thus, complaints that we misinterpret Arendt or that we don't consider other aspects of her work or other books of hers are misplaced and irrelevant.

[8] Cf. Volosinov (1973) argues that language should be essentially understood as dialogic therefore involving speech rather than as abstract structural sentence.

("products of thought") are reductive of worldly experience to thought.[9] Hence, as argued previously (Studdert 2006), Arendt's aim in THC is to re-configure our approach to *our* social. She reminds us of something the neo-liberal West, in particular, seems to have forgotten, namely that individuality is itself a communal construct, endorsed and maintained communally (Foucault 1975).

So while Foucault and Arendt share the same objective: the undermining of the sovereign humanist individual through the primacy afforded it within Cartesian and post-enlightenment thought, their mode of doing this is radically different. Foucault concentrates upon the rational individual as an historical manifestation of the state and governance. As such he does not really address commonality outside the state and governance except as an effect of governance, it is not his object. Indeed as many commentators have observed (Fraser 1987; Butler 1997) there is no place within Foucault's analysis for the creation of social being-ness outside the state/individual axis precisely because there is no alternative source of subjectivity. In contrast, Arendt locates herself absolutely in commonality and undermines the more fundamental Cartesian split between the world 'inside' and the world 'outside'; a split which bears within it, the concurrent expulsion of the individual from any role in the construction of the social world (Studdert 2006; Villa 1996).[10]

Arendt thus recreates the pre-Cartesian world by reinserting the communal origins of the social world back into the social world (King 1974), as well as through her renunciation of individual sovereignty. Thus her re-configuration undermines the Cartesian split between consciousness and the world of abstract social process, the mechanistic model, the

---

[9] Of course, Arendt does not oppose thought per se, simply the manner in which Platonic and Cartesian thought pre-constructs the social for us on every level as the *outcome* of thought. Against these abstractions, Arendt continually asserts the action of lived experience, the primacy and particularity of experience; yet, simultaneously, she also stresses the crucial social being of existence and even more crucially, the inter-relationality of experience.

[10] That this binary opposition, with all its powerless conceptual furniture, still informs social science analysis can be seen clearly even now, for instance, in the work of Giddens. In his 1999 Reith lectures entitled 'Runaway World', he postulates a binary opposition 'between the "out-there" world dynamics of globalisation and the "in-here" effects on our worries and sensitivities' quoted (with approval) in Girling. Loader and Sparks, 2000.

essentialised individual and its modes of instrumental reason, as well the regime of modernist knowledge derived from it (Studdert 2006).

So, how does she achieve this? As explained in more detail elsewhere (Studdert 2006, Chapter 7), the key characteristic is that sociality is an inter-relational action, in which elements are inter-linked, qualified and activated by the simultaneous presence of other elements present. Thus, action is qualified by the terms of plurality: the 'sum' of all the elements within each action of sociality.

Within her account, labour, work and action have both passive and active conditions; they express our nascent possibility and are shaped in turn by the world from which they emerge and fall back into and which is the only forum for their expression. Thus, any outcome cannot be derived wholly from either materiality or a pre-given subject in the singular, but can only exist as a combination of all.

Clearly the stress in her account falls therefore upon the linkages; which can be theoretically described as mutually constituting; a step which allows Arendt to avoid privileging any single element. Furthermore, each element has a conjoint positioning within thought, practice and space: a relationship to both the world of human beings and to the world of materiality (Arendt 1958, p. 23). This positioning, as will be shown, allows historical specificity- something crucial in establishing the non-essentialist status of Arendt's examination.

Let us now briefly define plurality. Firstly, plurality exists by virtue of the simple presence of others: that is its passive meaning. Secondly, the active mode is encompassed in this quote: *the simultaneous presence of innumerable perspectives and aspects in which the common world presents itself and for which no common measurement or denominator has been devised. For though the common world is the common meeting ground of all, those who are present occupy different locations within it, and the location of one can no more coincide with the location of another than can the location of two objects*' (ibid, p. 57). So the active form of plurality is 'interest'. Here taken, as with all other terms, in its widest sense as simply presence, expectation, self-description. 'We can never see ourselves clearly' records Arendt (op cit) and interest here is not presented as 'truth', rather as incomplete opinion in need of common ratification.

For Arendt, plurality is our common, social world: the world where it is impossible not to act (ibid). We are all born into this commonality, this pre-existing plurality, into its forms of communal sociality and into the materiality, which constitute it and which precedes and survives us. What is crucial about this is that while it clearly offers a critique of a pregiven rational unitary subject (Henriques et al. 1984), it is also critical of the assumption, which we discussed in Chapter 1, that the complex production of subjectivities is entirely dependent upon the discursive realm which, in post-structuralism, is entirely created in the technologies of the social. It is precisely the point we are trying to make that the common world has been excluded from such accounts. Conversely, by re-instating inter-relationality back into our picture of the world, Arendt locates her gaze directly into a world common to us all equally.

Arendt is clearly here, trying to think of being-ness in a non-sovereign, worldly way (Villa 1996, p. 118) and as such she seeks not simply to construct an oppositional logic, but to re-configure our understanding of our own social world (Curtis 1999, p. 16).

For labour, work and action exist within the world of human being-ness, they are both the actions and conditions of human being-ness, actions which shape and are shaped in turn by the world. They are activities through which systems of thought become concrete but which also exist as particular action(s) prior to systems of thought and prior to the individual (Gergen 1994, op cit, p. 27).

In turn as action and as speech as action, the *vita activa* illuminates the conditions under which the social human being-ness is enunciated.

Each of these human conditions has a conjoint positioning within thought, practice and space, which is in relation both to the world of human beings and to the world of nature (Arendt, op cit, p. 23). What is more, this positioning is subjective and objective, as well as historically specific.

Let it also be noted here, that this definition of plurality does not assign 'truth' to individual perspectives, as is the case in the contemporary casual use of the term. Rather than saying everyone has their own perspective, their own 'aspect', their own truth, Arendt simply acknowledges their multiple presence; a much more subtle approach. As such 'Truth' only exists as a temporary unity of all perspectives, held, implicitly or otherwise by, and as, a social agreement in common; not in each individual perspective. This will be a useful notion when we come to think about communal power. Truth is thus inter-relational and dependant on *us*, not 'me' or 'him' or 'her' or 'it'; something which applies equally to being-ness, and this 'us' is constituted by co-operation and agreement within the social as a whole.

Plurality is the world we enter and engage in as a necessity of survival. Yet while this ascribes us with presence, it does not, by itself, automatically assist our achievement of a *specific* being-ness. That can only be created equally as an outcome of our human action and our common acknowledgement. Personal being-ness can only be created communally; as an outcome within the common world.

The importance of action/sociality is noted in Arendt's claim that action is the exclusive prerogative of [humans], 'the single quality which cannot be imagined outside the society of [humans]' (ibid, p. 22). 'Action is the space where I appear to others as others appear to me, where humans exist not merely like other inanimate things but make their appearance explicit (ibid, p. 198/199)'.

Sociality therefore as common action in public, is always *potentially* revelatory: meaning, always *potentially* beyond the simply expected (ibid, p. 179). So it is through sociality that action reveals being-ness. It is through action that we show ourselves to others and are seen by them in turn.

As we act in public, our being-ness emerges through these actions and is recognised and sustained communally as 'who we are', as 'who I am' and as 'who you are'. Sociality in this world is therefore a ceaseless action of becoming 'common', our being-ness always a jointly constructed being-ness: 'I recognise you' and 'you recognise me'. Or to put it another way, 'I contain you and you contain me'.[11] And this being-ness is temporarily present to ourselves and to those around us, in the grand, in the small, in the mostly mundane micro-social actions of our lives; at once accessible, present, ephemeral and, in its totality, impossible to perceive.

---

[11] Obviously such an approach to recognition is in opposite to Althusser's assumption that all recognition is misrecognition (Althusser 1969). This stems from an important difference between her tradition and the French one in relation to the nature of knowledge.

Beyond this, there is simply no 'truth' concerning who we are. Yet it is, 'who we are'.

Public action thus cannot help but create relationships (ibid, p. 189) and through this, shared perspectives; sociality as action must always create public space, space in common.[12] For this I-ness, this being-ness, we manifest through each and every action of sociality and through each other, is seen, created, and endorsed in turn; contained, sustained and verified continually, simultaneously, by the presences of others (ibid, p. 57). And we do the same for them through our entwined role, as I and other.[13]

By locating being-ness as deriving from joint action in common, Arendt thus stands in contra-distinction to the more familiar anti-metaphysical tradition stemming from Nietzsche. A tradition characterised by what Yar (2001, p. 61) terms, a 'shared assumption of the objectifying and alienating character of secular intersubjectivity'. A tradition which links Lacan, Heidegger, Althusser, Sartre, Foucault to Hegelian notions of 'coming into self-consciousness' and 'a general belief that the subject is constituted out of modes of mutual subjectification, objectification and instrumental reason' (Honneth 2001, p. 161).[14]

---

[12] Here it is important to grasp that we are using the two wider of sense of action postulated within the Human Condition (pages 204-206 of Studdert 2006 explains this more clearly). These two wider senses of action are explained by Arendt: Firstly, in company with all other activities and conditions (Arendt 1958, pp. 7–9) it is a passive condition established at birth, forever linked to the capacity of beginning that natality embodies (ibid, p. 177). Secondly, as an actualising activity, it is creative as we shall see, of man's unique identity, human relationships, and the bridging of the objective and subjective worlds (ibid, p. 196).

[13] As Studdert explains (2006, pp. 204–6) Arendt nominates three versions of action. In the relevant pages of *Conceptualising Community*, he discusses all three and argues why it is that he adopts only two of them.

[14] This difference in perspective is vital. One manifestation of it being the differing approaches posited by Arendt and the French tradition (of which Foucault is a part) towards the relationship between agency and structure. It is often claimed that Foucault's work engages only with subjection/subjectification (the condition of being a subject) and not subjectiivity (the experience of being subjected) (Henriques et al. 1984). Others have argued (Fraser 1989) that he collapses agency into structure, effectively denying agency any role. Studdert argues (2006) that this manoeuvre is repeated all through that strand of anti-metaphysical work and arises, precisely from the notion of misrecognition, for example, as used by Althusser. Arendt, conversely, locates being-ness in common as an outcome of the inter-relationality of personal interest and the wider social world as expressed through the action of sociality. Thus, in her account, agency is not simply collapsed into structure, nor is structure subsumed by agency. Rather, the two of them sit as forces of containment

While Arendt's work is every bit as fervent in its rejection of metaphysics as this alternative tradition, it does benefit from her social viewpoint. In her account there is no *single* determining source of communal or personal being-ness, be it governance, the state, materiality or agency. Nor is her account of communal being-ness based upon any prior assumption concerning the terms of inter-subjectivity. Furthermore, in her account, there is never a complete, fixed 'I' to oppose any other complete, fixed 'I'; for the 'I', and indeed the 'other', are never essentialised, temporalised, closed or complete or, indeed, ever entirely separable.

There *is* only *us*, the commonality of sociality, the inter-relationality of action and the commonality of being-ness it creates.

This is a commonality mutually enunciated through action, not through fixed states of subjectivity. Arendt therefore inaugurates a different way to view the social: one in which the social and the common can be studied inter-relationally as moving fields. This can be achieved with ease, once essentialist and normative abstractions, individualist psychology, materiality, the state/individual axis, the primacy accorded terms like globalisation or networks are dispensed with at the investigative stage.

The second key characteristic present in sociality as action is that action creates more actions, more effects, none of which can remain under the control of its initiator. Action is thus uncontainable and unfinalisable (Arendt, op cit, p. 190). It cannot be closed or finished, even in the smallest matter. Effects remain unknowable, inherently open ended, creative of further actions, none of which the original doer can ever fully control or anticipate.

Containment of Action

Yet the first paradox is that something so central to human being-ness is also the most conditioned, most inter-relational, most constrained of Arendt's nominated activities (Studdert op cit 2006, p. 150 and Arendt op cit 1958, p. 178).

---

and action, one unto the other. The being-ness in common that emerges is therefore, in its temporality, always some combination of both.

We have now discussed the first aspect of action: its endless existence as the means for the revelation of being-ness, along with the manner in which this being-ness is established as 'truth'.

Previously we spoke of action as unfinalisable. Arendt speaks of fences and promises as exemplifying the sort of social checks and boundaries erected to curtail this unfinalisable aspect of action (Arendt, op cit, p. 191). What she termed 'Remembrances' (op cit, 208). The most crucial of these remembrances, however, are not fences, nor promises, but the fact that all actions of being-ness revelation, take place within a pre-existing, common world. The common world functions as the means for containing this unfinalisable quality of action (ibid, p. 137).[15]

All social formations perceive the need to limit the possible effects of action; all communal formations exhibit means of doing this: rituals, legality, custom, language, institutions and linguistic categories: rearing practice, madness, parricide, and so on (Auge 1999). However, these words often highlight exceptional cases; for a social science analytic, the exceptional is not our fundamental interest.[16]

Which brings us back to sociality, for every action of sociality in public is a simultaneous process of action/being-ness creation and action/being-ness containment. This occurs because the being-ness created through action is held inter-relationally, communally, through different perspectives tacitly and temporarily agreed upon; because 'truth' is established in the presence of others; because they confirm our being-ness to ourselves while we confirm theirs to them; something which is true, whether it is two people or thirty thousand.[17]

All actions of being-ness creation take place within, and fall back into, this pre-existing world of communal understanding—Arendt's 'remembrance': the world which existed before our birth, and which outlives us (ibid); this is the world in which we exist.

---

[15] 'The impact of the world's reality upon human existence is felt and received as a conditioning force' (Arendt 1958, p. 9)

[16] Or at least it shouldn't be. However, as Girling et al. observe (2000, p. 9), 'there would seem to be a tendency in some recent social theory to dramatize and to focus on the extreme poles of the argument.'

[17] 'An individual's utterances in themselves possess no meaning precisely because there is no source for that meaning. We are always positioned vis-à-vis others and the world' (Gergan 1994, op cit)

Our actions in this common world: the world of pre-exiting communal linkages, must relate to that pre-existing world.

This world of communal understanding contains all so-called subjectivity and all, so-called, objectivity and materiality. Whatever being-ness is created through action is therefore necessarily enunciated as a temporary, jointly constructed, union of the specific, the general, the particular and the common. The revelatory quality of action, the quality Arendt terms 'miraculous' (ibid), is therefore always contained and marshalled by the common world from our very first moment, moulded into a form that the common world itself can recognise. And this 'acknowledgement', no matter how temporary, must be present in every single action of sociality.

This common world, of course, also has a manifested material form contained in buildings, locations, speech, history, habits and practices, legal frameworks, economic 'realities' and customs. To enter any building, for instance, is to enter into a communal interaction, to have ones being-ness created inter-relationally through a temporary, jointly constructed, union of the specific and the general. Something easily illustrated by observing others and oneself entering different kinds of spaces, a twelfth-century cathedral, a family home, a football stadium on match day or a suburban London Off-licence at five to eleven, on a Friday night.

Once again, containment should not be seen here as a word with any connotation. Or rather it should be seen in its widest sense. It is the common world into which new actions of sociality fall. Containment of action functions in many modes simultaneously. All these elements are required to create, maintain and enhance recognition of the meaning arising from the unique action of being-ness creation enacted through sociality. Containment here is not therefore a value judgement or an abstraction, rather it is an exact description of the inter-relational eternal mixing, of action and the common world, within public sociality.

This analytic therefore hinges upon an examination of the particular *terms* of this inter-relational construction of being-ness, the terms of the engagement of action/creation and action/containment within any specific instance of sociality.

At this juncture, Arendt's account wanders down the road of her own interest.[18] She begins attaching value to certain actions over others, culminating in her famous account of the specifically political as the purest action (ibid). It is demonstrably and richly coherent, and will, in due course, prove useful to this account; from the perspective of our approach to community analysis, however, it is far too narrowly focussed, too value-laden for the analytic being developed here[19] (Studdert 2006, p. 200 note 7 explains this in further depth).

What is important now is to demonstrate how we might use this approach to understand communing. To explore how the analytic might help us in understanding our own sociality requires at this point, however, some interrogation of our fieldwork.

Sociality in Market-Town

Let us examine some instances of sociality and test the notion of sociality as the cockpit of being-ness held in common; we shall do this by utilising our research in Market-Town.

Introducing the Track

The first interview comes from a working-class couple in their late 60s who live on the estate. Initially she draws the route they walk down the hill, through Crawley Park, to Tesco's supermarket.

---

[18] Just to be clear, we are developing Arendt's account of the construction of social being-ness in a manner and for a task which is perhaps compatible with Arendt's intentions, perhaps not. Once we have outlined her account of the construction of social being-ness and borrowed two barely developed concepts from her work: the space of appearance and the web of relations, this is the end of her input. After that, we're on our own and whatever the outcomes, the blame, if any, is ours alone.

[19] Indeed, it is one of the basic propositions of this approach that all social formations are communal, or to put it in a simple example, that the state itself is a community manifesting communal being-ness in different strengths for different participants; that likewise the market is not a single totalised entity but, rather, is composed of infinite actions of sociality, and similarly that all other forms of collective action are created and sustained through the eternal action of social being-ness. This is hinted at in Arendt's account but never explored.

This is the common track for all of the estate inhabitants whenever they walk into the centre of town. This route will feature extensively in our data; it breeds commonality as much as it exemplifies it.

Two or three times a week this woman and her husband have a set route and pattern of activity, one which lasts from 9.30 in the morning to around 2.00 in the afternoon, when they re-unite and adjourn to Wetherspoons for a pint.

What the interview makes clear is that this routine is centred around and motivated by the need for sociality and being-ness creation.

I: *So, would you arrange to meet people, or it just happens that you see people you know?*

R2:   *Well, we do separate in town, she goes to Primark, and then she just rings me.*

R2:   *Where are you?*

R: *You know, she is going around the charity shops.*

I: *So, what do you do while she is going around the charity shops?*

R: *I go and look at my shops, you know, I like to browse in Smiths, you know.*

I: *Yea.*

R: *And ere, I just help her with her shopping, carries her bag, around there, and Wilkinson's that kind of thing, you know, and then ere...*

I: *And meet people.*

R: *Well, that's it, that's what we do as we are walking.*

I: *Yes, that's nice, isn't it?*

R: *And then sometimes we will have a pint after, you know.*

R2:   *He does [laughter].*

R2:   *Like I say, when I go to the charity shops I do meet people I have never met before, and we have a good natter.*

And later one she expands a little in response to a question.

I: *Yes, and so, if you met someone in the charity shop, who you didn't know, and you got talking to them, is that a way of making friends? I suppose that's what I'm asking.*

R2:   *Well.*

I: *Or just having a chat.*

R2:   *We just have a chat, you know, and they will tell you about them,*
       something, and feel as though you have known them for a long time,
       even though you have only just met them.
I: *Yes.*
R2:   *We just talk and that, but I do meet a lot of people who I went to school*
       with and, you know.

We raise several issues in relation to this transcript:

- Sociality is more important than shopping.
- The highlight of these trips is the chance to talk to strangers.
- The woman also talks to familiar people, people as grounded in the town as she is.

So here we have a situation of sociality, action in public, where being-ness held in common is both create and affirmed. And this action can only take place precisely because they are already aware of their commonality and recognise that commonality in others.

This one woman, she was talking to me for ages and she said, it's nice to have somebody to talk to, because she was a bit lonely, and we were talking for ages in the charity shop, and she really enjoyed it.

In all of this certain, shops could be understood as playing a strong role in bringing people together. They contain the unfinalisable effects of action, helping form and structure the sociality in a particular manner.

As such, the being-ness that exists within the charity shop is a co-operative being-ness, particular to that space; a being-ness created through the action of conversation and finally, a being-ness held in common; both by the other woman and by the husband present during the interview. To which we can probably include some of the people who work regularly in the shop and undoubtedly know this respondent.

This is a commercial space, but these people are not consuming anything. They are using it as a social space where one can meet people. In this instance, therefore, the terms of the materiality are shaped by the terms of the sociality taking place within it. In this example, the space of the charity shop becomes a meeting place in which strangers are able to talk to each other and, through this sociality, create a joint being in common, which is shared and welcomed by each.

I   So, just name a couple of spots on this map where your friends live.
J1: Oh my God, I could mark them all. Yea, they are everywhere, honestly, they are everywhere.
I: And do you see these people regularly?
J1: Yea, I bump into them in town, if not they will Facebook me, or send me a message, how's it going, you know, and that type of thing, I don't think I have got so many down towards, [the hospital] I know a few people down there, and I say hi to them there, but I don't invite them to my house, and I don't know invited, well I would get invited, you know, if I dropped a hint, but I wouldn't want to, but I do see them, but a lot of them are all over.

J1 a woman in her 40s lives on the estate and works as a volunteer at the community project office located on the estate. Throughout the interview and sustained by our observation within the office, J1 is known and knows a vast number of people in Market-Town. Indeed, she feels valued and praised for this as the interview reveals. She believes this allows her to talk to people on the estate in ways others can't. In a later interview, she stresses again her being-ness as someone who is known by everyone, as someone who has been around and is just like them.

J1's being-ness is created and held communally. But J1's being-ness has not only to be seen publicly, it also has to be recognised, agreed and held publicly in common.

Yea, that's what G** used to say, is there anyone in Market-Town you don't know? I mean, if I go off for the day with her, hiya, bump into people, hiya, she will go, oh my God.

This being-ness can be understood as a communal being-ness, an outcome of co-operative agreement in the manner suggested earlier in this chapter.

Conclusion

Both these examples contain varied elements. What is common to both of them, however, and what we want to stress here, is that all these 'lives' are self-described as the outcome of a generalised series of actions of sociality, encounters creative of further being-ness creation through action. This process is described by the speaker in the course of more sociality, taking place with the interviewer/stranger/researcher. At every stage, action within sociality creates meanings and again being-ness; all within the mediating prism of existing meanings.

These people construct their temporary being-ness through action in public with others and this being-ness is sustained within the combined co-operative meaning derived from these momentary actions of sociality. Thus it became possible to establish a social, inter-relational account of the creation of being-ness. We would argue that such accounts provide the basis for an inter-relational account of communal being-ness as a communal subjectivity held in common.

It is the constant repetition of these actions within boundaries of meaning held co-operatively, which is the outcome of 'two or three times a week' or someone constantly saying 'hiya' to everyone.

And this is because repetition creates meanings; meanings not exact in every way, but close enough for us to be able to describe them as meanings-in-common.

In the next chapter, we move on to discuss the means for thinking analytically about how to investigate sites where particular being-ness-in-common is produced.

Bibliography

Althusser, L. (1969). *On the reproduction of capitalism: Ideology and ideological state apparatuses*. (G. M. Goshgarian, Trans.). London/New York: Verso, 2013.

Arendt, H. (1958). *The human condition*. Chicago: University of Chicago Press.

Auge, M. (1999). *The war on dreams* (trans: Heron, L.). London: Pluto.

Bachelard, G. (1964). *The poetics of space* (trans: Jolas, M.). Boston: Orion Press.

Baker, D., Epstein, G., & Pollin, R. (Eds.). (1998). *Globalization and progressive economic policy*. Cambridge: Cambridge University Press.

Bateson, G. (2000). *Steps to an ecology of mind: Collected essays in anthropology, psychiatry, evolution, and epistemology.* Chicago, IL: University of Chicago Press (2000 reprint. First published 1972).

Butler, J. (1997). *The psychic life of power.* Stanford: Stanford University Press.

Curtis, K. (1999). *Our sense of the real: Aesthetic experience and Arendtian politics.* Ithaca: Cornell University Press.

D'Entreves, M. P. (1994). *The political philosophy of Hannah Arendt.* London: Routledge.

Foucault, M. (1975). *Discipline and punish.* Paris: Gallimard.

Fraser, N. (1987). Communication, transformation & consciousness–raising. In Calhoune, C. & J. McGowan (Eds.), *Hannah Arendt and the meaning of politics.* Minneapolis: University of Minnesota Press.

Fraser, N. (1989). *Unruly practices.* Minneapolis: University of Minnesota Press.

Gergen, K. (1994, May). Exploring the postmodern: Perils or potentials? *American Psychologist, 49*(5), 412–416.

Giddens, A. (2000). *The third way and its critics.* Malden: Polity.

Girling, E., Loader, I., & Sparks, R. (2000). *Crime and social change in Middle England.* London: Routledge.

Henriques, J., Hollway, W., Urwin, C., Venn, C., & Walkerdine, V. (1984). *Changing the subject: Psychology, social regulation & subjectivity.* London: Methuen.

Honneth, A. (2001, April–June). Recognition or redistribution? Changing perspectives in the moral order of society. *Theory Culture & Society, 18*(2–3), 43–57.

King, P. (1974). *The ideology of order.* London: George Allen & Unwin.

Marcus, G. E., & Saka, E. (2006). Assemblage. *Theory Culture and Society, 23*(2/3), 101–106.

Nancy, J.-L. (1991). *The inoperative community.* Minneapolis: University of Minnesota Press.

Ostrom, E. (1990). *Governing the commons: The evolution of institutions for collective action.* Cambridge: Cambridge University Press.

Sewell, W. H. Jr. (2005). *The logics of history: Social theory and social transformation.* Chicago: University of Chicago Press.

Studdert, D. (2006). *Conceptualising community: Beyond the state and the individual.* London: Palgrave.

Villa, D. R. (1996). *Arendt and Heidegger: The fate of the political.* Princeton: Princeton University Press.

Volosinov, V. I. (1973). *Marxism and the philosophy of language* (trans: Matejka, L. &Titunik, I.R.). Cambridge, MA: Harvard University Press.

Yar, M. (2001, April–June). Recognition & the politics of human(e) desire. *Theory Culture & Society, 18*(2–3), 57–77.

Part II

Developing the Analytic and Exploring Market-Town

3

Plurality and the Space of Appearance

Having confirmed Arendt's account of the creation of being-ness through actions of sociality, the next step is to develop an investigative analytic based upon that account. That is, a social scientific analytic designed for the investigation of *social* activity (Studdert 2006).

In Chapter 1, we discussed how theoretically 'community' functioned as an object of knowledge.

Chapter 2 discussed how Arendt's approach allowed us to develop an alternative account of the social construction of being-ness in common.

This chapter offers the second stage of the analytic for the investigation of communal being-ness. It establishes the first of two analytical tools appropriate for this task.

The Track

The track described here refers to a route walked by the people from the estate, down the hill, into the town. Everyone from the estate we interviewed marked the same route on maps of the town. It is a recognised thoroughfare.

© The Author(s) 2016
D. Studdert, V. Walkerdine, *Rethinking Community Research*,
DOI 10.1057/978-1-137-51453-0_3

Given the lack of shops on the estate, the lack of doctors, dentists or other services, it is a track well traversed. There is no pub or post office on the estate. Even to get the three different types of council recycling bags requires a walk down the track. Given that there are only two shops, many of the walkers upon the track are going to or coming back from shopping in the town. The track is walked by people of all ages, sometimes all the way to Tescos and town, sometimes as part of a path to somewhere beyond.

The track itself is about a quarter of a mile in distance and has two loose forms: the first begins at the southern edge of the estate, passes between some houses on a crescent, passes through the main Market-Town park, across the vast council car park, and culminates at the traffic lights on the ring road, before entering a paved shopping prescient running through to the main shopping street of the town. The second strand runs from the hillside portion of the estate, down the old Millford Road, past the high school, culminating at the northern end of the shopping precinct opposite Tescos.

The route itself is evidence of the exclusion casually imposed upon the estate by the rest of the town; however, what is prescient to our aims here is the importance of familiarity, the continual meeting of people 'like you', as well as the truth that this walking route provides the main axis for the emergence and participation of the estate in Market-Town life.

We have used the term 'The Track' as our shorthand. There was no name given to this route by the participants. This route is invisible on Google maps and cannot be found with a GPS tracking system. Nor is it known by the rest of the town: those who live in the commuter suburbs or the centre of town. In interviews, people from those locations, when they did mention going to the northern part of the town, exclusively describe venturing there by bus, car or simply walking up the main road.

Other elements of the town, therefore, do not attach any value to the route at all. For the town it is not even a whole, it is split into portions: Paul Crescent, the park, the pedestrian lights; portions which are not even aware they *are* portions. Only the estate sees it as a unified entity.

How do we think about the social space constituted by this track?

The first thing to say is that this space is constituted entirely through the actions of the people from the estate acting in common. This is a space which belongs to the estate and which winds deep into the town centre itself. As such its meaning is distinct and particular for those who use it. The entire track has a meaning, not even available to those who live outside the estate along its route. It is constructed entirely within the communal subjectivity of the estate.

Here is one couple, tracing the route on a map and describing it to the interviewer:

I: *And meet people.*

R: *Well, that's it, that's what we do as we are walking.*

R2: *We always go through the park like.*

R: *What we do, we just go along and then there is a thing, a bridge there.*

I: *Oh right.*

R: *The railway used to be there, and we go under this bridge, down through there, and then into the park, go through the park, and then we are into the town, aren't we?*

R: *Yea, so we go through the park, you can come out of the park by here, and then we go through the car park and, you know, then get into town that way, and then walk home the other way.*

I: *And people that you meet, are they just other people who are doing their shopping?*

R: *Yea, people coming up and going down.*

Her responses are beautifully described and re-lived in the telling. It includes locating aspects of history and memory: *the railway used to be there*, and it shows how one of the activities is simply meeting people: '*Well*', *that's it, that's what we do as we are walking.*

The description is thus clearly matched with the one quoted in the last chapter concerning charity shops and meeting people there. People, not necessary friends, but all the same, people like her.

Conversely another respondent, N1, recounts how she cried every day walking down the track to her school, in the first few months after her family had been re-located to the estate from Henry St in the middle of town.

Both examples show how lived experience is enmeshed in this route.

Given that N1 moved up to the estate from Henry Street in the late 1950s, it is clear that the track itself dates from the gradual establishment of the estate. It exists as a response to the lack of services and the geographical re-arrangement of living space by the county council.

There is clearly, therefore, a sustained communal being-ness being created here. It contains history, subjectivity and being-ness in common held within the physicality of the actions and the materiality of the space. Such communal being-ness augment already existing communal being-ness, and it is therefore easily incorporated into the overall communal being-ness particular to the estate.

At a later stage of our project, we commissioned a young estate woman to paint a mural on a wall adjacent to this route. It was a long, large wall, and she worked from 10 am till 10 pm for seven nights to complete it. During that time she was regularly joined by various people using this route, coming from town or going to it. Sometimes couples, sometimes friends, would stop for an hour or two, sit round on the grass, admire the mural, talk or paint some portion. Some of them brought alcohol; some had shopping bags and groceries. The fact that they were passing up the hill allowed the mural itself to become a space for sociality and therefore for the appearance of a being-ness held in common.

How do we understand this track, simply and clearly as a nameless space in which social processes continually occur? How can we investigate something both intrinsic to Market-Town, but containing as well, a unique meaning for the people from the estate; a function and role invisible to the rest of the town?[1]

The sociality of greetings and conversations exchanged by people walking up and down the track, the brief comments, is reinforcing of an existing estate identity; as is the bridge (which now isn't there) and the notion that it is an organic loop contained in the phrase *then get into town that way, and then walk home the other way.*

Across the divided road, at the end of the main shopping street, opposite the supermarket, is a taxi rank where the loop is completed; where

---

[1] Our notion of the track is distinct from the notion of 'desire paths', as discussed, for instance, in Hampton and Cole (1988). A desire path (also known as a desire line, social trail, cow path, goat track, pig trail or bootleg trail) can be a path created as a consequence of foot or bicycle traffic. Clearly, this is not limited to foot or bicycle traffic. Our view of this path is much wider. The track is simply an example. Something which becomes clear through the chapter.

people from the estate laden down with multi-coloured plastic bags take a cab home with their shopping. Fittingly, in light of what we have spoken about concerning the supermarket as an element in the track, the cab rank always has a queue of shoppers waiting, talking to each other, complaining, recounting; whining, and laughing—rain or shine.

How do we think of this track and indeed about social spaces like Tescos and more crucially, how do we conceptualise them inter-relationally?[2]

Space of Appearance

Firstly, given that spaces like the track are ephemeral spaces, constituted exclusively through action, created each time slightly differently and ultimately held only in common, how can we think about them; particularly given they are everywhere and are created not simply by materiality or one act of subjectivity or indeed by one person or one action of sociality, how can we think about them?

The term Arendt uses for these sites of particular sociality is the *space of appearance*: 'the space where we appear to others as others appear to us' (Arendt 1958, p. 199, 220ff), whether it be, for instance, a meeting, or a passing on the street or a classroom or a recording studio.

A space of appearance can thus be any size: this track, a football stadium, your own street, Facebook pages or transactions in a shop. It is the space created by focus groups, for instance, or a one-to-one interview or a space online, like a Facebook page. Finally, there are clearly multiple spaces of appearance within larger spaces, such as at a football match or a music festival where there are areas within that location which are in themselves spaces of appearance: backstage; dressing room; press box.

---

[2] We recognise that Arendt's concept of space is different from that adopted by such commentators as Massey (2005), and Lefebvre (2002), and these approaches always consider space as a contested terrain. However, in our example, the track is not contested. Rather, it emerges from the sociality of the people who use it. It is true of course that planners created the estate, so there is an element of power in the entire necessity for the track, but our point is that to analyse it *only* in these terms is to miss something much more fundamental. This space is an expression and creation of communal being-ness. The track expresses existing commonality but does not define that commonality or function as its exclusive space. Thus the track, as an element in that commonality, is both sustaining of those independently constituted communal meanings. It expresses those communal meanings and further develops and recreates them.

These are spaces of appearance within the bigger space of the stadium or the live music site. As such there are, within this notion, infinite spaces of appearance. Indeed everything functions as such as long as sociality, the act of appearing to one another 'in public', occurs within it. It is entirely through the action of sociality, the presence of people together, that this space of appearance comes into being. It is thus not an essentialist designation, for the very same philosophical reason that sociality cannot be an ideal or privileged form. Nor does the space itself have specific pre-emptive or inherent value in the manner, for example, of the concept of 'civil society' (Cohen, 1994 pp. 84–85).

By itself in isolation, the space manifests nothing; when there is no one present, it is not a space of appearance. Nor when it becomes a space of appearance, is it isolated from other spaces or dependant on some pre-existing binary relationship in the manner of, say a 'temporary autonomous zone' (Bey 1991) or the 'Commons' (Ostrom 1990; Ostrom and Hess 2007). Rather, it takes its status exclusively from the presence of sociality and any actions in public taking place within it. The space of appearance is, therefore, offered as analytical tool through which the particular means and terms of sociality creative of being-ness in common can be charted. However, that is not to say that spaces cannot leave ghostly traces in the landscapes of their formation. The concept of deep mapping (Deep maps: liminal histories and the located imagination. *Journal of the Imaginary and Fantastic, 2*(4)) alerts us to the fact that material remnants of former spaces might still exist, and that these can have an enormous power in the memory and imagination of the people for whom they acted as a space of appearance. Indeed we have already seen such in the respondent's reference to the railway that has now gone. We will discuss effect of such spaces in Chapter 6.

What we can say here is that any space of appearance is the common world; particularised as a single created space for the purpose of analysis. As such, it contains all commonality, without any single element having an exclusive defining role.

Action is what we know of the world, the public world gathers us together in a non-sovereign interrelated manner and thus in so far as it is common to all, signifies the world itself to us (Arendt, op cit, p. 80).

It does this because every space of appearance displays a combination of commonality and particularity, just as sociality does.

Thus, according to this approach, the track is precisely such a common world, a meeting ground; one where people are present to each other. By using the track and crucially by recognising it as such, those present create and share in a being-ness in common. Moreover, it is creative of a social space in which 'we are'.

Actions of sociality are performed in the space of appearance, and the space of appearance functions as the arena for creation of being-ness in common which is the outcome of the linkage between action and containment, generated through sociality.

What this analytic is fundamentally tasking itself with, therefore, is to provide the capacity to undertake an examination of the specific terms of the particular creation of being-ness as they inter-act provisionally to produce commonality from the action of sociality.

It is an analytic which examines the terms of the containment of action and the construction of social being-ness. The space of appearance specifically provides the means for both inter-relationality and the terms through which in commonality emerges as an outcome of action and containment, to be seen.

The Household and the Polis

Arendt offers two particular exemplifying instances of opposing spaces of appearance that illustrate her point concerning the different terms for the creation of being-ness: these are the polis and the household (Arendt 1958, p. 152). A brief examination of these will assist us in understanding some central issues around this element of our analytic[3].

The polis is postulated hypothetically by Arendt as free of any consideration of personal benefit or advancement flowing from decisions made within it, thus allowing the communal being-ness to manifest pre-

---

[3] It is important to remember that in her account of the Polis and the household, Arendt is offering examples of the two space of appearance as a means to examine the creation of being-ness in common (see Arendt (1958 p. 152) and Hansen (1993) for the reasoning as to why these are exemplifying spaces). These examples are created by the terms in which the creation of social being-ness is actioned and contained.

dominately from the aspects and actions within the immediate action of sociality. Whatever emergent being-ness in common appears, has shaped itself from the specific actions of the social encounter. The Polis is open to a plurality of all possible meanings, with the outcome held co-operatively and agreed in common. The being-ness that emerges from this commonality is infused with the primacy granted to the immediate commonality and action within the space of appearance—it is aware of its own requirements and conditions (Studdert, op cit, p. 154).

The household is the contrasted space. Here the space is ruled uniformly, the emergent being-ness is predominately the weight of imposed meaning originating from 'outside' the immediate sociality; it represents the weight of containment. In the example Arendt uses, this containment is performed by religious authority, filial authority, custom and practice (Arendt, op cit, p. 27, p. 28). This authority 'fills' the space of appearance and dictates the terms for being-ness creation. The independent possibilities of action are severely curtailed. In our contemporary world, this role can be performed by legal frameworks like health and safety, state violence or surveillance, and normative demands or custom.

For Arendt, these are exemplary instances. They sit for explanatory purposes in a binary opposition, along a horizontal continuum. In the lived experience of sociality, the line is far more blurred, and examples of this blurring are commonplace; the balance between action and containment is never clear-cut and neither element is ever totalised or totalising within the space of appearance.[4]

Let us explore this briefly using Tesco supermarket as an example of the household.

In her interview, P4 recites the script given to her by Tescos, which she is required to recite to every customer as a condition of employment.

P4 describes the script as follows:

---

[4] This is where we depart from Arendt, who, while nominating the space of appearance as something open to everyone, nominates the polis along with political action as the highest form. The reasons for our departure are outlined in Studdert (2006, op cit, pp. 150–154). In reply to those who believe this departure represents an overturning of Arendt's ontology, the reply is that we are using Arendt's approach to develop our own analytic in relation to community, not slavishly adhering to it. There is no requirement for us to follow every word of her script, whatever our admiration for her work.

Hiya. Do you need any bags? Would you like a hand with your packing? Can I do anything else for you, that sort of thing. It's a great day. Have a nice day.

As Arendt observes, the household excludes possibility of action and instead expects kinds of behaviour. To which end it characteristically imposes innumerable and various rules, all of which tend to 'normalise' its members, to make them behave, to exclude spontaneous action (Ibid, p. 41).

The following example is offered to show two things: firstly, to serve as an instance of the attempt to impose totalising rules akin to the household across the space of Tescos as a whole. Secondly, to show that such an imposition is never, and can never, be totalising. That action within the space of appearance always works to complicate the simple imposition of household rules from outside.

P4 states that she has 'lots of friends all over town':

I: *And when your friends come in, and you say the script to them?*
P4:   *Mmhmm.*
I: *Do you laugh?*
P4:   *Sometimes yeah, I just try and go off a bit, go off the track a bit with them [laughter] and I talk for ages.*

Later in the interview P4 tries to justify this departure from official script.

I think with other people, sometimes you just go unnoticed, when you are going through the checkouts, and things like that, but I think it's nice to be noticed, and for somebody to want to talk to you, instead of just throwing all your things into a couple of bags and sending you on your way.

So here we have one space of appearance: Tescos composed of smaller spaces of appearance, such as P4's particular checkout.

She reports that the best thing about the town is her friends, and the worst thing about the town is her friends. Their action in appearing at her checkout precipitates a being-ness held in common which serves as a check upon the unfettered working of the script as imposed action.

Within that wider space of appearance, there are obviously smaller spaces of appearance happening simultaneously: for instance, P4's interaction with her friends is occurring simultaneously with other checkout workers having their own interactions with people. The being-ness in common varies for each of the encounters, and each space of appearances is created by the particularities of the encounter. The intention of the household is to regulate the construction of being-ness in common, to make it literally uniform, and to do so, through control of the space of appearance. This is the script's entire purpose. However, despite all the aspects of control imposed on the space of appearance, there is no ultimate capacity for power to control every space of appearance or indeed, every manifestation of being-ness in common. Control of the space of appearance varies from site to site and is subject to time and other elements. It is more pervasive in, for instance, call centres; much more so than in chance encounters on the street. What is clear is that even within household situations, control of the creation of being-ness can never be totalised.

The power of the household, in this case Tescos, remains overwhelming within that space of appearance, but it remains provisional.

Using the polis and the household allows us the means for comparing the terms for the creation of being-ness within different spaces. In the case of the track, for instance, we could understand this as being close to Arendt's description of the 'polis' in that it is a free space where people interact willingly without interest. However, in 1958, Arendt saw the polis in rather narrower and more overtly political terms than we are doing here (ibid, p. 201). She used examples such as 1956 Hungarian workers' councils (ibid 215–17). For the purposes of our analysis of community, we would propose that we use the term to illustrate how a space such as the track is the coming together as social action and being-ness in common. To us, what is important in Arendt's account are the terms under which being-ness is created as an outcome of the space.

We think this is the fundamental proposition of her work and her examples, which we must remember are two contrasting instances, are not presented here as the only categories for understanding the space of appearance.

In the case of the track, as we mentioned, we see it as a relatively open space for the creation of being-ness. In the case of Tescos checkouts, however, all though it is circumscribed in the manner Arendt ascribes to the household, we should also note that many participants in their interviews also considered it as a space for meeting friends. As one person put it, 'I spend hours shopping because I am always meeting people.' Thus, we are adapting Arendt's notions to allow us to think inter-relationally about communal being-ness. The space of appearance is a simple generic term which allows the development of an investigative analytic. In the final section of the chapter, we analyse one example of a community project office to demonstrate the usefulness of the analytic beyond these two polarities in describing inter-relational social space.

Spaces of Appearance in Market-Town

This section of the chapter extends the analysis by exploring the complex inter-relation of household and polis in one location, the estate office of a government anti-poverty programme. The aim is not to present a fully formed analysis of the office but rather to show via two small examples, the capacity of the concept of the space of appearance to examine the terms for the creation of being-ness in common. The concept of the space of appearance thus allows us to see how being-ness is formed inter-relationally.

The government anti-poverty intervention scheme is located in a street-front office on the estate.

The office is a single fronted, ex-retail shop, sitting between the only butcher and the only other shop on the estate: a family off-licence. There is a small parking space outside for six or seven cars.

The office is busy from opening to close. Various people who were consistent volunteers estimated that the office received about 1000 people a week. The space is full of volunteers; the desk is always peopled by two volunteers at a time. Some of these front desk people are doing unpaid work experience.

The back rooms are often used for unscripted chats or meetings, the weekly credit union and other activities timetabled in advance. The receptionists deal with questions, direct people around the building or ring upstairs for the two professional paid workers: L1 the manager and G4 the office manager. L1 is present frequently in the building but is usually in his office in the far corner of the top floor. G4, on the other hand, is ever present around the desk.

In the small reception area, there are always people; conversation flows continually, as does laughter. Only the very old do not appear. People come in for the credit union, for jobs, for the after-school club, for computer classes, to use the computer to write a letter, to see someone, to seek advice or just to say hallo. The chair of the local housing association, the biggest on the estate, drops in, says hallo, has a query and leaves. The office space itself, at any given moment, is generally disproportionally female.

J1 confirms the way in which this office functions as a central element in the estate.

I: *And how many people do you think are on this estate, just roughly, like half, or a quarter, or three quarters, or whatever, of the people who live on this estate come into this office, and use this office?*

J: *I would say a good half.*

I: *And are they all people that other people know because they are kind of related to them, or are they just strangers?*

J: *Everyone knows everybody.*

Clearly this is a space of appearance; a space where being-ness in common is routinely created and sustained, a site of sociality that exists within existing communal linkages and being-ness.[5]

For us, it offers a more complex example of the inter-relationality of different elements conjoined in the ongoing creation of being-ness in common.

Thus, in this example, the being-ness in common that emerges does so as the result of a more blurred inter-relationality. What we discovered in fact was that there are two versions of what 'in common' means, and that

---

[5] As an aside, we would claim that this sociality, *on its own*, does more to create and sustain community cohesion, than many of the agenda-driven programmes, ostensibly, the official task of the centre.

these versions sat uneasily, side by side. One was the government agenda, and one was the estate's notion of its own being-ness in common.

The national funding body presents one model for the creation of social being-ness in common. In this model, individual aspiration was the key for the estate to move out of poverty into improved health, improved skills and, in particular, into education.

Two views of the world met at the front desk, and it is indeed questionable whether the government had any notion of the estate as anything other than a collection of poverty-stricken individuals.

What we discovered within the office, within this single space of appearance are questions and differences over commonality of purpose and questions which hindered the production of being-ness in common. The inter-relational, unspoken, conjunction of these differences, regarding exactly what the commonality of purpose consisted of, meant that the being-in-common of the office, the project and the participants was hindered in their overall task of assisting the estate.

This disagreement existed much more on a vague level of uneasy and a vague sense of the failure of possibility. It emerged in small instances, several of which we will now describe as examples of the flexibility of the notion of space of appearance and its capacity as the means for examining the inter-relationality of all the elements involved in the construction of being-ness in common through sociality. For this reason, we will not examine each example in depth, simply point to their presence.

First Example

Our first example is a 31-year-old father, here called R1. R1 is clearly focussed on work and finding work, one of the services the programme aims to provide.

As expressed in the interview, this man's entire identity is bound up in his notion of himself as a worker. He speaks in the interview about being recognised in pubs because he's known as a good worker—'everyone will talk to me.' He shows the interviewer pictures of a wall he just built; he mentions that G4 encourages him and publicly describes him as a good worker, which pleases him greatly. Originally, he tells us he comes from an inner city working-class suburb and moved to Market-Town to marry a woman. He dreams of moving to somewhere near Heathrow, 'his mate's place' where he knows he'll get a job: 'there's plenty of jobs at Heathrow all the time.' He clearly has a fixation on this, even though his wife won't move and he currently can't afford a car to look for work or attend out of town interviews.

A volunteer, N8, is helping him write his CV. Writing CVs is almost a magic elixir for these schemes. No matter which community centre you attend anywhere in the county, at any given moment, someone is writing a CV. G4 is clearly seeking to help this man. He is praised around the office, and his work is on the computer for G4.

Yet after two weeks he disappears completely and is never seen again while the CV is left unfinished. 'We've still got it stored on the hard drive,' says G4.

The basic issue appears to be an incompatibility between notions of what constitutes work. As described in his interview, R1 has a very particular idea of work, one he undoubtedly shares with the communal being-ness of the estate. Certainly it is an idea which many progressivists, political or otherwise would describe as 'old-fashioned' or 'a hindrance'. R1 has had work before, lots of it, but the only work he wants is outdoor work—agricultural work, picking potatoes is one he nominates. He tells us he can't work in factories that they are 'too cramped'.

We thought it telling that R1 was one of the few post-25-year-old males to venture into this office. Many of his contemporaries from the estate are by now, at least informally, regarded by programmes like this, 'as too far gone, too lost'. Most of the younger men like R1, if they come into the office, perhaps to get something signed, which happens occasionally, usually present with a rather sullen kind of attitude; certainly they are affronted with the notion of being clients. Between their view and the view of the intervention programme, there exists a perpetual mistrust, which in interviews comes over as a grudging truce for extraneous purpose (Walkerdine and Jiminez 2012).

For understanding this we need to think inter-relationally about the notion of work propagated and served by the programme and the office. Within that programme space, the notion of work is of service industries and low-paid positions in shops following scripts or in some office doing clerical work, jobs that require a CV. Within that space, R1 simply cannot find himself or his sense of being-ness in common. From the programme's perspective, there are many reasons why they can't accommodate the being-ness of R1. You could say, for instance, that the programme is not an employment agency. Indeed the variety of work they prepare or train people for is actually a rather narrow palette. So the CV sits on the hard drive and when the office closes nine months later, R1 has still never been seen again.

The second group of people we can perceive inside the space of appearance of the office are the volunteers. In Chapter 7, we deal with this group in more detail, all we want to point to now are the on-going issues between professionals and the volunteers which are undermining of the required commonality of purpose.

A7 is a volunteer, a frequent visitor to the centre, who lives on the estate and is very well connected to a large number of families through friendship and kinship. A7's view as articulated in interview is clear: the office was built for the estate community and should be used to help this community. She has a view that the community and the government organization should work together as equals.

When present in the office, either as a visitor or a volunteer, A7 will often give advice about government legislation and practices to the waiting people from the community, either people she knows or just the ones who have told her casually their problems or situation. This advice often involves who the person should go to see and their addresses or phone numbers.

This practice of A7 is highly frowned upon by the paid office manager G4, who claims she is anxious about possible legal consequences. She has told A7 not to do this on a number of occasions, a dictate A7 routinely ignores.

A7 is also part of an informal local community association composed of local residents who attempts to support estate people by organising, for example, coffee mornings, bus trips and fund-raising. In due course, we will examine the outcome of the simmering conflicts between this group and the 'owners' of the office.

Thus, using the space of appearance in this manner allows us to locate specificity within the actions of sociality, creative of being-ness in common within one space. It frees us from the sort of normative accounts which, despite their best efforts, routinely ascribe essentialist designations to individuals: won't work, shirkers, left behind, hard to reach, and so on, and allows us to see the local issues pertaining in this particular space. Being-ness is never static no matter how apparently solid its inscription upon a person may appear to be.

To study something inter-relationally requires an inter-relational account of the construction of being-ness. Only such an account serving as the foundation of investigation, can free us from examining both the state and the individual as if they were monolithic designations. Despite their differences R1 did attend the office for a short period and A7 does acknowledge the importance of the office for the estate.

So none of these disagreements are aired in an overtly conflictual manner; nonetheless, it is clear that these versions of being-ness in common are incompatible in key points and, moreover, that this incompatibility can be investigated because it emerges from an accurate understanding of the inter-relationality in the office. It thus allows us some understanding of the issues undermining the overt aim of the programme - an undermining that contributes to the perceived failure of these interventions principally, because the difference between these notions of what in common means is never clear. Therefore, being-ness in common becomes difficult to create and sustain; it is fractured in ways that undermined the best intentions of the community members and, indeed, of the paid staff.

Of course, this incapacity to fully achieve what the volunteers hoped could be achieved is also reinforced a notion of the estate as incapable of helping itself.

Thus, using the notion of the space of appearance allows us to see clearly how the inter-relationality of all the elements is at play within the space and to do so in a manner which moves beyond current debates, for example, Lefbreve's work on space (2002), Rose (1999), and Rogerly and Becky (2011).

Plurality in the Space of Appearance

This chapter has been dedicated to explaining the concept of the space of appearance, and then showing how it provides a means of investigating the terms for the creation of social being-ness in a particular social space. We saw how thinking via the space of appearance allowed us to understand the track in its inter-relationality, allowed us to understand the terms under which Tescos sought to create the being-ness in common between its staff and customers, and finally, how confusion around commonality restricted the terms of the social being-ness constructed in the office of the estate anti-poverty programme. All these accounts build upon the inter-relationality of elements within the space of appearance and use the space of appearance as an analytical tool to understand this inter-relationality.

This final section shows how the terms of plurality within the space of appearance can both create and restrict the terms for the enunciation of being-ness in common within a space of appearance.

Again we will use the space of appearance provided by the office of the government's anti-poverty programme.

What this example illustrates is that the terms of the active plurality within a space its degree and variety, is itself an inter-relational element in shaping being-ness outcomes for the programme.

Plurality and the Anti-Poverty Programme

Our interview data revealed a town which, if not actually divided on a formal level, nonetheless functioned within self-imposed boundaries creative of a divided town. This notion of a divide was much stronger in the town itself and in the more middle-class commuter suburbs. These areas clearly saw themselves as the core of the town and showed little if any interest in the estate. People from these parts of town colloquially and commonly referred to the estate as 'the reservation'.

From the estate's perspective, their lack of shopping and services forced them to be present in the town particularly in the daytime. This presence, this physical access to the town, however, in no way amounted to any form of equal access to the resources or indeed the political processes of the town, formal or informal.

There are many examples of this, most of which we will deal with in due course, and the aim here is simply to note the divide as it is presented in the data.

Of course, there is one very real difference between the older town and the estate: the older part of the town does not have an anti-poverty programme; it is not judged to be a poor area using the deprivation measures common to national funders.

Therefore, simply by its existence, this well-intentioned programme confirms the divisions between the town and the estate. Nor is the town council averse to using this difference to informally divest itself of any responsibility for the estate.

A recent 65-page future plan for the area including Market-Town contains a section entitled 'No-one to be left further behind'. In that section, there is a paragraph relating to the estate:

> *The ending of the anti-poverty programme has brought into sharp focus the need for some form of continued effort to co-ordinate the provision of services targeted at the most vulnerable and disadvantaged communities.*

In the entire 65-page report, this was the only mention of help or assistance for the estate. What the anti-poverty programme has achieved therefore is to effectively provide the town and the county with an easy 'out' in relation to their responsibilities to the estate as part of the town.[6] This status is further reinforced by the description of the anti-poverty

---

[6] For the estate, the situation is further complicated by an administrative decision to locate the estate in two different jurisdictions: one belonging to the town and one to a northerly adjacent parish council. This administrative demarcation occurs despite the obvious fact that there is no physical break between the town and the estate, the estate sees itself as part of the town, most of the residents were born in the town and all of them depend on the town for their basic needs. Furthermore, the parish council itself is largely a fiction: almost all its council members reside in Market-Town or on the estate. What such a demarcation does achieve, however, is to further distance the town council from any responsibility for the estate, while of course preserving the estate residents as consumers in the town; the only role they are effectively allowed to perform. Yet the people on the estate feel united with the town as one community and are indeed demonised by the town as one community.

programme on the relevant government website where the structure of the programme is detailed:

The programme has anti-poverty officers which between them work with all of the communities eligible for inclusion in the programme.

In this simple statement, the linking of the words 'communities', 'programme' and 'eligibility' appears to confirm the particularity of estate as something distinct from the town, implicitly confirming in the minds of the rest of the town the division they already believe exists between them and the estate.

All of this places the volunteers and the staff in the estate office in a limiting and damaging role-one that impacts their capacity to achieve anointed tasks.

For what this policy of exclusion from the town means, in practice, is that while the government intervention office is, as we saw, positively reinforcing of the estate's idea of itself, to itself, the presence of the office as part of a programme applicable only to the estate is, simultaneously, re-affirming the estate's own implicit difference from the town. Further, this status is restrictive of the estate's access both to town resources and to the political processes of the town itself. The effect of this divide constrains the work of the intervention programme in subtle ways.

G4, a long-standing worker in community offices of this kind across the county, reported in our interview that

R: I don't think the voice of the estate is heard. I think there is not enough volume in their voice there's not much weight in their voice . . . it doesn't seem to hold much.

She then goes on to add:

Especially working in xxxshire there's a lot of knowledgeable people, a lot of perceived middle class people, lots of skills, and those seem to be the ones who are listened to most.

Further in the interview, she discusses the various day-to-day tasks that the office is meant to provide:

We've been asked to report on the number of people going for computer courses who have now got a European Computer Driving Licence ECDL now they can better access to the Internet or now they are more employable because they've got this qualification. But what about the people that are coming who are stressed.

I: *Right.*

R: *The people who are coming that need some advice there and then.* <u>*For people coming in who needed their CV done because they need to submit it by three O'clock because there's a chance of a job.*</u> *(our emphasis) We've got to do all that. We can give them some certificates, we can give you some experience and we can write you a reference which not everybody can have. You have to find a professional person for a reference, I don't know anybody who is a manager or a teacher.*

Getting references signed, compiling CVs are skill shortages and employment blockages at a very basic level.

Denied the plurality that engagement with the town could offer, being-ness for the inhabitants of the estate can, in these circumstances, only remain confined to the estate. The programme thus inaugurates a social being-ness which simultaneously creates and re-creates both the 'positive' enhancing aspects of being-ness in common; and its mirror opposite: the image of the estate as under-resourced, under-skilled and adrift from the real world, in short, a 'reservation'.[7,]

The particular terms of the plurality within the space of appearance constituted by the office thus creates a social being-ness both reinforcing of the estate while concurrently confirming both to the town and to the estate population its own exclusion.

For instance, the absence of solicitors is something that could be solved with a roster built around the participation of the solicitors of

---

[7] Furthermore, this attitude of the town is in defiance of the fact, reported by a local housing association chairman, that the majority of the houses on the estate are now privately owned. So in fact the identity applied to the state by the town is utterly out-dated at least in regard to government housing.

the town. This would allow people who need references to at least find someone capable of providing them. We are not saying this is a perfect solution but it would at least begin to solve an obvious problem. Unfortunately nothing of this sort ever occurs or indeed was ever proposed, as far as we know.

At a later point, G4 comments upon this lack of linkage between the office and the town when she says,

> *More often than not the relationship between the community and the service providers is a closer relationship in the more affluent suburbs. The run of the mill kind of community would have a relationship with recycling, street cleansing and street lighting and maybe car parks in town centres … but not much of an impact on much of a relationship with the police, the social services, with the school, I think we find that developing those relationships in the community especially with the school and police by the community here is difficult.*

While G4 speaks here of this lack of linkage in terms of service providers (some of which have a rather spotted relationship with the estate community in any case as we shall see), the lack of linkage 'enjoyed' by the estate with the entire town, *including* social services and the police, seems not to occur to her. In short, the town had no particular presence in this office, nor did it seek one.

What this example does show is how the creation of a being-ness held in common is shaped inter-relationally by the absence of immediate actionable elements, that is, by the particular terms of the plurality and the particular terms of action and containment that is present within the space of appearance.

Thus we can see how the space of appearance as an analytical tool allows us to see the inter-relationality of all elements, both evoked and unactioned within the space of appearance. Further we can see how this inter-relationality in its plurality of elements creates being-ness from the specific terms in which the elements are present or 'absent' (absent meaning, in this sense, non-actionable).

We propose that this analytic and the notion of spaces of appearance allows us to examine the production of social being-ness in common in a comprehensive manner and allows us to see how the inter-relation of elements like differing views of commonality, the type of space, and the terms of plurality, all impact upon the form of the particular being-ness in common produced within that space.

We have now given a social account of the creation of social being-ness and have developed an analytic which allows us to investigate the terms under which particular creations of social being-ness occur. We have shown that commonality does not produce uniformity, but rather manifests differently in particular instances. Crucially, we have located our investigation as an investigation of the terms creative of being-ness in common.

The next chapter will examine this last example of the Main Street on a Saturday in much more depth when introducing the notion of Meanings-in-common.

Bibliography

Arendt, H. (1958). *The human condition*. Chicago: University of Chicago Press.

Bey, H. (1991). *The temporary autonomous zone* (trans: Wilson, P.L.). Autonomedia (New autonomy series). London.

Cohen, J. L. (1994). *Civil society and political theory* (pp. 84–85). Cambridge: MIT Press.

Hampton, D., & Cole, D. (1988). *Soft paths: How to enjoy the wilderness without harming it*. Harrisburg, PA: Stackpole Books.

Hansen, P. (1993). *Hannah Arendt: Politics, history and citizenship*. Cambridge: Polity Press.

Lefebvre, H. (2002). The production of space. In M. Dear & S. Flusty (Eds.), *The spaces of postmodernity: Readings in human geography*. Oxford/Malden: Blackwell.

Massey, D. (2005). *For space*. London: Sage.

Ostrom, E. (1990). *Governing the commons: The evolution of institutions for collective action*. Cambridge, UK: Cambridge University Press.

Ostrom, E., & Hess, C. (2007). *Understanding knowledge as a commons: From theory to practice*. Cambridge, MA: MIT Press.

Rogaly, B., & Taylor, B. (2011). *Moving histories of class and community: Identity, place and belonging in contemporary England.* London: Palgrave.

Rose, N. (1999). *Powers of freedom.* Cambridge: Cambridge University Press.

Studdert, D. (2006). *Conceptualising community: Beyond the state and the individual.* London: Palgrave.

Walkerdine, V., & Jimenez, L. (2012). *Gender, work and community after deindustrialisation: A psychosocial approach to affect.* Basingstoke: Palgrave Macmillan.

4

Meanings-in-Common

Introduction

The previous chapters described the production of communal being-ness and the analytical space—the space of appearance—through which being-in-common emerges in its particular specificity.

In Chapter 2, we established that the unfinalisable nature of all action required a means of containment. This was because it took place in the common world and required that common world to sustain its being-ness. We argued that containment was always present in the action of sociality itself. It follows that being-ness, emergent from any moment of sociality, must, therefore, be held in common. In that sense, it can only come into 'existence' through others. Thus, commonality is a pre-requisite for the validation and maintenance of the being-ness created through sociality.

This chapter investigates how being-ness-in-common is held co-operatively and sustained and recognised over time. In other words, it explores how commonality builds its own capacity for 'recognising' itself. To do this, it requires the introduction of the idea of *Meanings-In-Common*.

© The Author(s) 2016
D. Studdert, V. Walkerdine, *Rethinking Community Research*,
DOI 10.1057/978-1-137-51453-0_4

This chapter explains this term; it shows how it fits into our investigation and how meanings-in-common can be interrogated as an investigative strand for understanding communal being-ness (community). Through all of this, we will be noting the role repetitive actions play in the creation of 'meanings-in-common'.

Meanings-in-Common

Earlier, it was claimed that sociality is an infinitely formed and continuous action, in which we are enmeshed day after day. As Gergen (1994) remarks, there is no other source of meaning than the common world, and we are always positioned in relation to it.

We proposed that all sociality is constructive of a temporary 'we' held in common by the collection of perspectives, and further, that this emergent social being-ness exists as a particular and ephemeral combination of the specific, inter-related elements of action and containment of action.

We argue that containment is necessary because action, creative of being-ness, is required to be recognisable to others. This requirement to be recognisable arises from a fundamental need for relationality and participation *in* the common world.

So crucially, this containment of action is what the common world itself exerts upon the particular action of sociality. The result of this is to bind being-ness in common and sociality within the common world.

The outcome of these actions of sociality is, therefore, one in which a temporary being-ness-in-common and a temporary meaning-in-common are produced jointly.

Being-ness becomes known through the placing of action within the common, joint experiences and prior meanings of the encounter as a pre-existent field already present.

In our account, therefore, 'meanings-in-common' are proposed as a relational field-one in which linkage produces the possibility of meaning, in a manner consistent with what Volosinov (1973) terms 'theme'. That is, the 'upper actual limit of linguistic significance', in contrast to the 'lower limit', which is the 'meaning of words in a system of language' (ibid).[1] In other words, what these words/actions express to somebody becomes more important than what they 'mean' in pure, definitional terms—their connotational or affective meaning.

So, for example, when people in Market-Town meet on the track, the meaning of the encounter is generated together and is distinct from, though clearly related to, what the track means in one person's biography. Of course, we know that meanings are created discursively and in forms of governmentality, but we are also claiming that they are created in the sensuous joint experience of the repeated walking, feeling and talking. In addition, the constant sociality is required for our own survival.

It is also crucial to understand that meaning-in-common has no meaning aside from that recognised in the action of sociality. Even 'remembrance' of action that lingers in the memory of the *communal* being-ness requires the continued sociality to provide its meaning. Meanings-in-common are about the action of recognition, and the action of acknowledgement, *in public*; they are about in *common-ness*.

The means by which meanings-in-common arise, are shared, and developed is illustrated by the following examples taken from our Market-Town data.

Small Actions of Communal Being-ness

We asked our research participants questions concerning their interaction with others in their immediate living area, be it a street or a block of flats.

Almost everyone interviewed reported interactions of help and assistance from or with neighbours in their street or block of flats. The following are examples of common types of response:

---

[1] In regard to Volosinov's notion of theme, we are in agreement with this description: "Illocutionary force requires already an element which is not narrowly linguistic, a social recognition of a standardized act (a promise, etc.). And in turn, these standardized illocutionary acts might be thought of as tools which are used in actual discourse to perform "macro-speech acts" at supra-sentential level. These acts are no longer a relative narrow and conventional set; they have to be related to concrete areas of discourse (i.e. to concrete areas of social activity). .... but 'theme' is still more concrete; it is not 'this kind of' macro-speech act, but this speech act being interpreted in this particular situation'. José Ángel García Landa 1988

'Yea, you know what it's like, being in a box, I'm living downstairs, and there is one woman on the floor, we all share, you know, we all look after each other.'
'Yea, yea, my street is a nice little street to live, the neighbours are as good as gold.'
'We talk to everybody, all the neighbours talk to everybody.'
'I think it does, it helps us all out by looking after each other.'
'She has magazines, and she will pass the magazines onto me. I will pass magazines onto her. Gardening books come to me, if I get any they go back to her, you know.'
'I don't have a problem, or if I need didn't have a tool for the car, or something like that, I would go and speak to one of my neighbours.'

These are social actions taking place between people who exist in close proximity to each other and are productive of being-ness held in common. They also produce a meaning-in-common. We can take this idea a bit further with the following example:

When my son was younger, he used to spend a lot of time in town, and getting on the bus, people would speak to him, and speak to me, and that feels nice, you are not ignored. It makes you feel like you belong. It makes you feel safe.

Here this parent reports the sense of safety and belonging created by simple repeated actions of strangers speaking to her son on a bus. Yet, the affects and meanings communicated are profound—belonging and safety, elements generally recognised as part of ontological security (Walkerdine 2010; Walkerdine and Jimenez 2012). Thus, we can propose that these exchanges between strangers, united in a space of appearance, are productive of a being-ness. It is productive of a being-ness in common and a meaning-in-common, which is partially, and importantly, a sense of belonging and feeling of safety. It also reminds us of the checkout woman in Tescos whom we met in Chapter 3, who believes that speaking to people helps them feel recognised and stops them feeling ignored.

In short, in both spaces: Tescos and the bus, these sorts of encounters are creative of a common 'we' that has a profound importance in our lives. Clearly, given that the respondents in both instances are speaking of past events in a generalised manner, this is a meaning which survives over time.

The major mode for this linking over time is simple repetition (Sewell 2005; Giddens 1984). Given that most sociality follows mundane, known courses, attuned to our need for social being-ness as a mode of survival, such repetitive small actions fulfil our need to sustain a stable notion of communal being-ness. It is no surprise then that the two outcomes listed by the mother on the bus are belonging and safety. Indeed in social being-ness, safety and belonging are simply two sides of the same coin.

It is also clear how, at a certain point, after prolonged repetitive actions of a similar sort, these meanings manifest as a shorthand understanding in the actions of our lives, our practices, our materiality and subjectivity.[2] Through particular encounters we develop a wider sense of being-ness in common and we act upon it. Thus, particular actions of sociality lead to being-ness held in common, creative, in turn, of meanings-held-in-common, that is, communal. This, in turn, produces communal being-ness in an active mode: active in the sense that it becomes understood to *some* degree.

I: *so if you go say to [the city] and you see someone there you know from*
        Market-Town do you acknowledge them, smile?
P1:   *yeah mostly I do. There's a kind of bond isn't there.*
P2:   *sometimes he even says hallo to people he won't talk to here.*

This is precisely meaning-in-common and communal being-ness raised to a form where the participants recognise each other in their commonality. Moreover, in the quote, the commonality is contextually specific and seen as distinct from individual likes and dislikes: *he even says hallo to people he won't talk to here.*

Having established that sociality as an action is creative of social being-ness through commonalities of meaning, in our research, we sought to investigate what could be done with that, and where, if anywhere, it might lead us in our thinking about 'community'/communal being-ness in Market-Town.

To show how we did this, the examples that follow are presented in a series of instances which expand outwards, not only in size—one street, the mall, the town—but also in degree of 'recognition; starting with a

---

[2] William H Sewell Jr.'s notion of eventful temporality (2005, p. 100) is moving towards the same position in relation to historical sociology. I admire this work but it lacks an account of the creation of social being-ness of the sort underpinning this analytic. As a result, despite Sewell's good intentions, his account is constantly hovering on the edge of a slippage back into abstraction.

neighbourhood, then a town, culminating with an instance where we consciously sought to use meanings-in-common to create a space for the 'enhancing of cohesion' which we define (unlike social capital) as 'increased communal recognition of meaning-in-common through aided increase in sociality'.

Examples of Meaning-in-Common

Neighbourhood

The previous section discussed small actions of sociality and their linkage through repetition to communal meanings held over time.

Here, in this first example taken from two narrative interviews, we move from the 'personal' to wider manifestations of communal being-ness, initially through data taken from the account of a middle-class male who resides near the town centre.

Despite the fact this respondent's work requires that he be absent five days a week from 7 am to 7 pm, the man's response addresses precisely the areas of meaning-in-common we seek to understand. In this example, we are moving from the 'immediate' to the more 'heightened' and augmented forms of communal being-ness.

Well, I mean, I think there are various levels, I mean we definitely have a community spirit in this terrace, I mean we are a terrace here of six houses, or whatever, or eight houses, there is definitely a community here, I mean we have been here twenty-seven years, something like that, erm but we are not the oldest here by any means, there are two other neighbours that have been here longer than us, some came at the same time, and some of the others are far more recent, and we do look out for each other, there is definitely a community sense.

I: And what would, in a sort of practical everyday sense, how would that manifest itself?

G: Well, we do help each other, I mean an example, a recent one, on the weekend I was sorting out some electrics in our bathroom, I ran into problems, and the fellow next door came around and literally solved the problem for me. On the other side, Susan is a music teacher, and a musician, she goes off, she has got a dog, and erm, we walk her dog, on the weekends, because rather than the dog going into kennels.

Here's another example of the same thing this time from a commuter suburb on the southern side of town:

Yea, no, it's like last summer, we did a street party, and it was successful, but then again, it was the same four or five persons doing all the printing, the leaflet drops, collecting them back to see who was interested, so we did all the organising, but we must have had about fifty or sixty of them turn up, so it can't have been that bad.

And it turns out that this busy woman also contributes to a community garden:

L: at the moment we are doing the garden, I don't know if you have seen it, by the library there.

I: Yes, I have.

L: I think that is the same group of us doing it, with a bit of help from the xxxx group, that's a youth group, and Keep X Tidy are helping us as well, we are doing all that together.

Street Scene

We wanted to see how these meanings-in-common existed on a larger scale and in a situation 'less personal' than one-to-one narrative interviews. We also wanted to illustrate how meanings-in-common can be held among a large group, the members of which do not necessarily have to know each other individually.

To achieve this we used an art-based method, involving an actor on Saturday morning in the main street of Market-Town, dressed in a dark blue velvet coat and a top hat, looking somewhat like Gene Wilder in '*Willy Wonka and the Chocolate Factory*'.

We provided the actor with a white, old fashioned wooden sign post, pointing in three directions. Behind the arrow tip on each prong was a blackboard slot where people were asked to write the names of the place in Market-Town they most liked, most disliked and most wished that the current town possessed.

Passers-by were approached and a steady stream participated. There were good reasons for thinking that the Saturday main street might reveal what people thought about their town.

The main street itself is a long south–north thoroughfare, stretching for around a mile to a mile and a half, running through the entire town. One way in parts, divided in others, pedestrianised in others, then again one way for traffic, and finally, leaving the shops behind, it curls across the small river, before ending after a row of suburban terraces, at a major transport junction, which marks the edge of town and the beginning of the A roads.

In the central shopping portion, it is a relaxed space, containing a divided road at the southern end, a pedestrianised mall section as it moves north and a narrow one-way street at its northerly conclusion. On its route through the shops, it is over hung with buildings of different 'ages'; a street with waves of traffic, rather than a stream. On Saturday from around 10.30 in the morning to 2.00 in the afternoon, people are everywhere crossing the narrow road, spreading out into its rather well-worn pedestrian mall.

Throughout this main street, from down at the bottom besides Tescos, where the street again becomes much wider, up to the other end of the shopping street where the pedestrian mall itself stops, leaking out among the paved pedestrian streets that run away at right angles from the main mall towards the post office and the main parking area; all through the length of this area, down a hill lined with shops—throughout this entire stretch—there are waves of people in tight, constant, multiple socialities: encounters, hallos, bustle, laughter and conversation.

People are ducking into shops, browsing, strolling, saying hallo, running and chatting; some people are struggling in crutches, some navigating on motorised wheel chairs. Families, pensioners; young people in groups; two men in their late 70s kitted out in 'squaddy' army greens, strolling, hands locked behind their backs, Monty style, as if they're inspecting the world before the battle. Like us they walk up and down among the crowd, while groups of various sizes and ages cling to the shop windows ignoring the displays, chatting loudly to themselves, while their children scurry and quarrel and pull at arms and clothing. As always, people queue outside Greggs, the cheap chain baker, while opposite, outside the closed Woolworth's building, the usual busker sings and people queue at ATMs and nearby stands the usual *Big Issue* seller, and virtually every Saturday the same punters are lounging in front of the bookies.

What we hoped this task would allow us to see clearly was the actioning of communal meaning in a larger, sharp and observable form.

This main street is a space of appearance, defined by its unfettered plurality of personal interest and tasks, and defining, through the creation of being-ness, the town's communal being-ness to itself. The presence of large groups of people within this space of appearance strengthens and acknowledges the communal being-ness within which the social being-ness of everyone is created. It acknowledges the plurality of the town and the random nature of it. It strengthens the notion that 'Market-town', in the words of one respondent, 'punches above its weight'.

Many of these people, particularly ones from the estate, who constitute the predominant group in the largely working-class crowd, come to shop, however emotionally, as in the example from Chapter 2, they have just as much desire to see each other and be seen, to relate to the town as a place where they are known, where their being-ness is acknowledged, allowed and confirmed.

Responses to the actor's questions ranged from the raucous to the whispered and people almost always consulted others standing around them, be they friends or family.

In the 140 or so vox pops (1 % of the town's population), there were a striking amount of opinions in common—in approximately 85 % of these interviews three kinds of statements stood out:

- The main street and shopping wasn't what it had been. Many mentioned specific types of shops that had come to predominate in the town: too many charity shops and too many hairdressers. Virtually everyone agreed with the opinion that 'the town had been going downhill rapidly for the last 20 years.'

- The town council was entirely to blame. They were 'incompetent', 'smug', 'distant' and 'closed minded'; 'they concealed information' and were 'unrepresentative'. They had allowed the town to run down, especially the main street. They had squandered opportunities and were only interested in themselves and in making money.
- Despite this, the town and, most importantly, the people in it, were 'friendly', 'fabulous' and 'warm'.

Often these opinions would draw nods and exclamations of support from the people listening. According to field notes, the phrase 'lots of people agree' was used in approximately 80 % of interviews.

While these views were generally held, among those over 40 years, in particular, there were also dissenting opinions which in themselves constitute meanings-in-common. Thus, many of the young people we interviewed spoke of Market-Town as 'dead', 'having nowhere to go', with 'no places to hang-out' and being a town for 'old people'. For this younger group, and they were well represented, there was a general feeling that it was a town they didn't want to stay in, that they no longer shopped in, and which required updating. Many parents agreed with these opinions of their children, particularly in regard to the lack of facilities for young people.

Finally, it is important to present the areas where people did not agree.

A lot of people disagreed about how 'rough' the town was. Many reported they would not go into pubs around the town—that they were 'dodgy' or had 'bad atmospheres'; many named one particular establishment as the 'drug pub'; others stated they wouldn't come into the town to socialise. One older gentleman casually remarked that there had always been 'punch-ups' in Market-Town, and spoke rather fondly, in this regard, of the town hall dances held in the 1960s.

One person, who identified himself as a recording engineer, came up to us and delivered a rather impassioned speech concerning the amount of drugs in the town and the hidden violence.

Many others took the opposite tack, praising the safety of the town, stating they always felt safe in Market-Town. Others said there was no more crime than there ever had been; that there was no more crime in the town than anywhere else; and that there was no place in the town they didn't feel safe.

These views are not presented by us as 'truth' or, indeed, as an accurate reflection of what the town is really like. They are simply offered as examples of meanings-in-common. They are meanings-in-common because they are centred upon the town and incorporate views about the town. So the comments which contradicted each other were often prefaced with statements such as, 'lots of people may disagree', 'lots of people think the same as me', and so on. Responses are framed within a collective discussion stemming from a collective perspective. Given that the questions were about their town there was a striving, not necessarily to agree, but rather to speak from a common ground to acknowledge other perspectives within a collective perspective. Thus, we are not talking of meaning or agreement in any simple manner, or indeed that meanings-in-common cannot be contradictory. What we are saying is that disagreement or contradiction is contained within a sense of commonality. Thus, the frequent claim that 'community' is a site of stifling conformity is from our data far too simplistic in its normative account.

It was also interesting to us that this commonality of meaning extended to the widespread repetition of extremely similar speech responses, phrasing and even intonations, as the recorded interviews attest. This commonality of speech crossed all forms from one-to-one interviews, to focus groups and to the sort of vox pop interviews being described here. This commonality of speech patterns, phrasing and words was also something noted in other sociological accounts (cf. Girling et al. 2000).

There were other meanings-in-common filling this main street Saturday-morning space.

One example is the informal roles and uses of the benches and seats which stretch along the main pedestrian mall. The ironwork benches at either end tended, according to the field notes, to be fully occupied by older people, mums and their children; these people moved on quite regularly and were promptly replaced by different people. The field notes record this as occurring constantly throughout six different Saturdays.

On the other hand, in Locke Square, in a portion of the pedestrianised walkway, there are wooden benches inlaid in the wall opposite the dry cleaners. These are also occupied all day, but for a much longer periods and by an utterly different range of people. This group tends to be much poorer, more mid-20s to 40s, bearing signs of alternative culture or older, quite poor working-class people, principally men. Small groups routinely gather around these benches and some people sat cross-legged on the ground, exchanging drinks, cigarettes and prolonged conversations. There was an air of permanence about their occupation of these seats, and the ground around the benches was strewn with butts. Many of the men had cuts and grazes on their faces.

The field notes record these benches as being full from nine in the morning till late in the afternoon; indeed, at times there seemed to be almost a hierarchy so that when someone departed briefly, they would simply return and reclaim their place.

These informal practices centred around shared notions, in this case, which benches are available for whom, for how long, for what purpose, and so on, all demonstrate meanings-in-common.

But these meanings-in-common are quite benign; the field notes record another, much more unsettling meaning-in-common: a group of nine persons, rather poorly dressed, a family of all ages from young children, to mum, to youths from 14 to 24, tightly huddled together, walking fast through the mall on this same Saturday morning. The young men in the group snarl and shout for no apparent reason, while everyone else, without exception or direction, literally make a teardrop shape around them as they passed by. The field notes record one of the steering committees identifying this group as belonging to one of the two families, who it is claimed are responsible for most of the crime and violence in the town. So meanings-in-common can also include conflict and indeed, the means of avoiding it.

Clearly from the almost unconscious behaviour of the rest of the shoppers, meanings-in-common operate here as well.

While we recognise there is much we could say concerning this last example, the reason for including it here is to demonstrate simply that meaning-in-common can take a bodily form and be widely shared without conscious agreement on the part of all those communally assembled.

The reason we have included several different examples here is that they are all recorded as having taken place in the same space of appearance on Saturday morning. They all show, therefore, multiple meanings-in-common of different strengths operating within the same social space. They all illustrate our main point, which is that being-ness in common binds people together.

The Meaning of the Open-Air Swimming Pool

One of the major issues that emerged from interviews was a set of strong feelings about the closing of an open-air swimming pool that was built in the 1930s by the then borough council.

Ownership of the pool fluctuated over the following decades between various forms of town, borough or county council. Originally, the pool was heated via a boiler and open for six months a year. However at some point in the late 1970s, the boiler broke down. The county council, who were by then the operating agent, refused to fix it, instead, passing control of the pool back to the town council, who, for financial reasons, were unable to repair the boiler and subsequently began operating the pool on a three-month, unheated, opening cycle. Subsequently in the 1990s, the town council closed the pool for financial reasons. It was finally demolished and filled-in in the first decade of this century, despite efforts by local community groups to keep it open.

Interview responses concerning the pool were couched in very similar terms across all town locations and classes. Very clear meanings around what the pool meant and the feelings about its demise could be understood in our terms as meanings-in-common. The main themes that emerged were happy times, family picnics, the joy of swimming, a cheap day out with friends and family, the community coming together, meeting people there and having time to chat, while their children played safely.

We offer below one example:

I: *And can you remember the swimming pool?*
R: *yeah, It was fantastic, you know, and that's where all the sort of poor kids were, in the park through the summer, sort of swimming and stuff, it was something to do, and it kept you out of trouble, you know.*
I: *Yea.*

N: *But I will always remember someone saying, you know, I was young at the time, and they said oh you will miss that pool when it's gone, and I said no I won't, because we have got the leisure centre, but you do miss it.*

I: *What's the difference between the pools?*

N: *Well, you had obviously, it was outdoor, and plus you had a lot of people going there and stuff, you know, from other families, whereas they don't go to the leisure centre because it's expensive, you don't see that many people there, you know, unless they are on some sort of fitness regime, you know, or they go elsewhere, like X [a nearby town], or Y [another town], if they can travel, you know if they have children, it's more fun, you have got slides, and you have got diving boards, whereas you had that at Market-Town, you had diving boards, and you had like a baby paddling pool, whereas you don't have that at the leisure centre, but the lady who run that supposedly she had a lottery win, I don't know how true this is, as I said I was only very young at the time, but she put her own money in to try and keep it going, so it was a great loss in that sense for the town, because there is not that many open-air swimming pools left in Britain as a whole, the only other one I know about, that I have actually been to is in XXXX, and that was a nice pool.*

After getting so many interview comments about the pool, we started to discuss it informally with people. We noticed that people immediately became animated, swapping personal experiences and stories, responding in actions and speech that were happy and joyful and full of movement.

This is when we began to understand that the meanings attached to this pool were meanings held in common. At this point, many years after the pool was closed, the pool was no longer the topic of any current action, rather it was shared among family and friends as a happy memory and as an ongoing complaint (one of many) with the council.

We started talking to town councillors informally about the pool and the reactions we had encountered in these interviews. Simultaneously, we tried to discover the history of its closure as well as the council's response and to speak to them concerning the communal anger at what had occurred around the pool, and the feelings of disempowerment regarding council decisions in general that it fed and nurtured. Initially, councillors were surprised when we raised the issue, often dismissing it with a wave of their hands. When they did discuss it, they opposed the interview concerns with their own account based on financial contingency, as well as citing the fact that the council had built a replacement leisure centre.

One councillor R2 summed up the general council opinion concerning the pool:

I: *When you came here was the swimming pool still open?*

R: *It still is.*

I: *No.*

R: *Oh no, you are looking at that one, yes, ere yea, just about I think, yea.*

I: *Yea, why did they close that?*

R: *Erm, health and safety I think.*

I: *Yea.*

R: *I think it was very costly, the town was running it, it was very costly to ere maintain, it was old, ere and of course, it was only open for a few weeks of the year, with the weather we have over the year, and you will appreciate it.*

I: *But it was a place where a lot of people could go, wasn't it?*

R: *Yea, I'm sure it was a magnet.*

I: *People took their kids during holidays, and the parents could take them down there, and sit all day.*

R: *Yea, yea, but we never used it.*

I: *No.*

I: *Okay, and what about the leisure centre, I mean a lot of people say, well, they like going to the leisure centre, but it's expensive and it's only open sometimes and you know, it's not, I mean I'm interested in kind of places where people gather.*

R: *Yea, Yea, I understand ere what you are saying, I don't use the leisure centre, my wife does, so she will be able to, she goes swimming first thing in the morning. I think you are going to get this erm everywhere, you know, with any services that are supplied, erm you are going to get a small minority that have used them, which means, to a certain extent, the majority are subsidising them, ere so from that point of view it is going to be ere expensive, now if you want the leisure centre to be open a lot more than what it is, then people are going to have to have an increase in council tax to pay for it, you mention that, and it's an immediate no, no, yea, we want it, we want it as cheap as possible, but we don't want to pay for it.*

This is a very different response from the discussion which appeared on our Facebook site:

Person 1:   *I hear the pool is closed, what a shame many happy memories I had swimming there. The characters I remember who worked there, xx and xx. Who's decision was it to close the pool? For sure that was a major mistake.*

Person 2:   *On a summer's day I'd call for x and xx and off we'd go down the "pool" for the day with our bathers rolled in our towel. We'd meet our mates in the queue outside and then head for the long changing rooms with our crates. We managed to fill the whole day somehow, sunbathing, posing, messing around. Saluting as we jumped off the top board and watching X swallow-dive off it! At the end of the day we'd stagger up to Mrs X's shop by the tennis courts for a Walls ice cream and then back up X Road, over the bridge, stopping for a rest before the climb up Y to Z Way—ready to do it all again the next day! XX saved my life too after I followed the bigger lads into the deep end! After jumping in and pulling me up from the bottom of the pool he put a towel around me for 5 minutes and then told me to get back in! We all had respect for the pool and for x and x, they let us have fun and we all stayed within the rules. Great, happy days!*

Person 3:   *Very, very happy days. Rescuing a brick from the bottom of the pool. Making a life buoy out of pyjamas. Oxo and a jam sandwich, and if you timed it right you got the crust! There'll never be another xx!! Councillors should be shot for knocking it down. Don't suppose they applied to the Lottery which has a special fund to save outdoor pools. The people of [Market Town] paid for it, and were never asked about saving it. Bastards!!!!*

Person 4:   *I used to have a season ticket every summer. There were always queues to get in every morning & afternoon. I seem to remember we younger ones had to get out by 6pm but the older kids could stay til 8pm.*

We could argue that the councillors were operating with one set of meanings-in-common, those relating to financial considerations in difficult times, while they failed to engage with the meanings-in-common presented by the interviews and Facebook discussions. In the town's meanings, a modern indoor leisure centre cannot accommodate cheap family days out or create the sense of communal being-ness, apparently generated by the open-air pool.

As researchers, it was our belief that the meanings-in-common about the pool shared some features that were about a material space of communal being-ness. If this were the case, then communal being-ness could itself be remembered without the actual pool being present.

We set about creating a free festival on the site of the pool – a site now grassed over. We set up stalls, competitions, paddling pool, teas, and so on. As the event gathered steam, the attitude of the councils changed markedly. At a council meeting attended by three members of the research project steering committee, the councillors vied to tell us their happy, personal stories concerning the pool. The county and town council gave us an empty brick wall for a mural and the space for the proposed pool day without question. The county gave in kind, principally by allowing their staff, who loved the idea, to prepare the wall for the mural and assist wherever they could. Increasingly, people and local organisations were coming to us: the friends of the park, the local newspaper, the fire brigade and local companies who donated £300 of building materials for the plastering and preparation of the wall.

The mural in the portion of the local park where the pool once stood was planned to feature images of the open-air swimming pool, surrounded by images of the town. The mural was to stare across what had become a rather isolated and neglected part of the park.

A young woman from the estate designed and painted a mural in ten days. Luckily, she knew so many people that from the very first, people simply kept turning up to help. One young husband and wife spent two days painting the left-hand corner. The mural became a hub of sociality, particularly for people on the estate, a supposedly hard-to-reach group.

The day itself was a spectacular success: attendance was very high, the fire brigade turned up to fill the ten paddling pools we had erected to suggest the environment we wanted, all while the fire fighters told us their own stories about the pool.

Fireman: I was born here and I learnt to swim here and so did my daughter B. Daughter, also a firefighter: I learnt to swim here. I loved it. It was always full and I miss that sense of belonging you know.

Indeed enthusiasm was so strong that the locals themselves began planning an annual pool-themed festival.

What it confirmed was the validity of our understanding of what meanings-in-common were, but it went further: a local councillor who opened the mural understood clearly the importance of the meanings-in-common and suggested an open-air paddling pool for children in the park space. In a sense, this also brings the difference between the council and community meanings full circle: the council recognises that the issue was not about the provision of a leisure centre but concerned the preservation and activation of a set of meanings about communal being-ness, meanings which bound the town together.

From our perspective, it was clear that simply creating opportunities for enhanced, relaxed sociality between local town folk was, in itself, creative of community cohesion. That this occurred through the generation from previous meanings of a new sociality and new communal being-ness, publically expressed through the construction of new spaces for sociality; new spaces which in themselves created more sociality and more expressions of communal being-ness.

By placing this event inside the town's usual web of relations, it establishes the potentiality for further spaces of appearance and new forms of communal action. For instance, some members of the steering group then went and established a community kitchen supplying cheap and wholesome food to people from the community.

Conclusion

Arendt's account of social being-ness has sat unexplored in her work for over 50 years.[3] One reason for this is that without the additional framework that we have developed of meaning-in-common and the linkages they establish to communal being-ness, her social account of the creation of being-ness remains simply *potentially* useful. By extending the implications of her account, we are able to not only find a much more productive and sophisticated means of investigating communal being-ness but also formulate a method for understanding the production and development of communal being-ness, in which the issue is not about how much capital a community has, but the possibilities arising out of the understanding of its own communal meanings. All space that is communal has such meanings. In other words, no communal space is 'community poor' in that sense. Hence, the central and signal importance of understanding communal being-ness in this way. In this sense, it is not about assets (Putnam 1993) or positive attributes; so-called negative meanings may be just as important in this regard as so-called positive ones.

Understanding meanings-in-common arising as an outcome of the creation of being-ness through sociality thus provides a more effective way to achieve what social capital strives for, but which in their case, results predominantly in big projects, the cohesive effects of which are incapable of being measured, accompanied by what amounts to subjective assertions concerning 'good' communities/'bad' communities; assertions which simply undermine their own efforts and indeed, in many cases, simply make disenchantment worse.

In the next chapter, we will develop the final part of our analytic.

Bibliography

Gergen, K. (1994, May). Exploring the postmodern: Perils or potentials? *American Psychologist, 49*(5), 412–416.

---

[3] Dana Villa (1996) is one exception here.

Giddens, A. (1984). *The constitution of society*. Berkeley: University of California Press.

Girling, E., Loader, I., & Sparks, R. (2000). *Crime and social change in Middle England*. London: Routledge.

Putnam, R. D., Leonardi, R., & Nanetti, R. (1993). *Making democracy work*. Princeton: Princeton University Press.

Sewell, W. H. Jr. (2005). *The logics of history: Social theory and social transformation*. Chicago: University of Chicago Press.

Villa, D. R. (1996). *Arendt and Heidegger: The fate of the political*. Princeton: Princeton University Press.

Volosinov, V. I. (1973). *Marxism and the philosophy of language* (trans: Matejka, L. &Titunik, I.R.). Cambridge, MA: Harvard University Press.

Walkerdine, V. (2010). Communal beingness and affect: An exploration of trauma in an ex-industrial community. *Body and Society, 16*(1), 91–116.

5

The Web of Relations

The previous chapter introduced the notion of meanings-in-common. We saw how meanings-in-common were the outcome of sociality, containment and action within a space of appearance.

Clearly, spaces of appearance manifest multiple, simultaneous meanings-in-common, meanings both implicit and explicit. Indeed, 'unspoken meanings' constitute the greatest proportion of what is manifested within any space of appearance. Further, every space of appearance intrinsically shares some fundamental meanings-in-common, for example, the need to communicate and create sociality in common as a necessity of survival.

We also saw how meanings-in-common, centred on the open-air swimming pool and previously shared only informally, could be gathered together to augment existing communal meanings.

To this point, therefore, we have the following investigative analytic: sociality in public = action + containment = being-ness in common/ meanings-in-common + repetition = communal being-ness.

This is the gist of our approach to the investigation of communal being-ness (community). The analytic is thus a simple one. The space of

© The Author(s) 2016
D. Studdert, V. Walkerdine, *Rethinking Community Research*,
DOI 10.1057/978-1-137-51453-0_5

appearance we discussed in Chap. 3 is the initial element; this chapter will discuss the final element: the 'web of relations'.

The *web of relations*[1] is Arendt's term for the totality of all human activity. However, Arendt only speaks of this in very general terms, "the common world of human affairs which exists wherever human live together" (HC1958, p. 184). Clearly, this is Arendt's way of discussing the common world as a relational and defined space of infinite complexity. The issue for us is how to develop it as the basis of an analytic for the investigation of communal being-ness.

Any analytic of this sort must show the means for linkage between particular instances and the wider web. This chapter will illustrate those linkages by using the space of appearance and the wider web while demonstrating how they link one to another.

Let us begin by describing our development and enhancing of Arendt's comments regarding the web of relations as the common world. The web of relations is the complete worldly space in which our own spaces of appearance form a minute portion. The web of relations is thus 'concerned with the matter of the world of things in which [humans] move' (ibid, p. 182). In short, this web is the common world (p. 52), and it contains everyone and every aspect and 'interest' (p. 50). Arendt further describes this web as the space that 'exists where ever [humans] live together (ibid, p. 184)'. It is the world of absolute plurality—acknowledged and unacknowledged—the world where the subjective and the objective intersect (ibid). Clearly, therefore, this web of relations is the world we are born into and which outlives us. It contains everything prior to the outcome of the immediate space of appearance but it is never still or fixed and it is continually altering, albeit in infinite minute ways. From this account, no single element is ever stable enough to be privileged in the creation of being-ness. Instead, it is the relationality of the web of relations and the

---

[1] This notion of a web has been picked up by many commentators (Rorty 1989, p. 41). Unfortunately, their continued attachment to mechanistic thinking, in combination with a perceived need to conform to state- and discipline-driven imperatives, such as the inherent primacy afforded the state/individual axis, has resulted in the word and the thinking being shoehorned into an impossible and debilitating framework incapable of incorporating hybridity, multiplicity and plurality the defining features of communal being-ness in this and every other age (Studdert 2006, p. 199 note 7 discusses Rorty's particular approach and criticism of it in more depth).

materiality in it that allows us to grasp the terms through which being-ness in common is made possible.

The following example illustrates in a simple everyday form, the inter-relationality of the web of relations and the space of appearance.

Our recent community research project (Walkerdine and Studdert 2012) was built around a steering committee composed of research-ers and local volunteers. At meetings, members of the steering group, together, decided all the 'whats' and 'hows' concerning future events. Of course, the meetings involved sociality and therefore multiple actions of being-ness creation occurring through the same process of action and containment described earlier. The shop-front office at the anti-poverty building was the physical space of appearance, while what Arendt calls the particular 'interest[2]' in common of the participants constituted the space where we appear to others.

When we came to discuss proposed events, one person drew on their knowledge of national health and safety legislation; another outlined her local contacts among the town hall officials and suggested who might help us; a third spoke of the national legislation pertaining to consent forms and ethics; another described certain approaches based on their experience of the town and how certain activities might be received; someone else spoke of certain people from the regional government who might be approached.

All this information was traded and exchanged, measured within parameters linked to the purpose. We then discussed, questioned each other, and contributed either with supporting information or alterna-tive accounts or silence. In short, people reached out from the space of appearance; we say 'reached out' because they did not leave the space of appearance, they simply, as it were, widen it to include things required

---

[2] In this context, for us, interest should not be considered as prior to relationality. It is relationality that makes possible that participation in a unique constellation of webs of relations. Yet even this so called personal view, is a meaning-in-common, an inter-relational outcome of action and com-monality. The particular inter-relational outcome derived from our entry into the world and our being-ness in the world. Interest therefore should not be taken to mean ability or something inher-ent, something outside the inter-relationality and plurality in which every aspect of our lives are jointly contained and created. Interest in this form is not therefore a collapse of agency into struc-ture because we are an *element* in the construction of being-ness in common and in the mainte-nance of its commonality.

by the common interest at hand, constructive of the space of appearance itself. This means that they widen it to bring into the space of the meeting, relational webs of meaning, knowledges from the wider web of relations, as and when it pertained to whatever common world we were discussing.

In this account, the web therefore opens/activates inside the space of appearance according to the demands of the space of appearance; it opens in a particular, specific, layered and partial form, drawn into the space of appearance, and shaped by the specific interest and demands within that immediate space of appearance.

The web of relations resonates implicitly in its entirety within every space of appearance but it is accessible only through the common interests of the participants. So the space of appearance is not enfolded into the web of relations (Rose 1999, op cit). Rather, it is the means by which we see particular action in its generalised context; nor can one exist without the other. In a real sense then, the separation is investigative and analytic, in our actions both are one and concurrent with each other in different forms: one as wider communal meanings and the other as particular interest: the same thing in short, viewed from different perspectives. And of course, these perspectives can change and as they do so in different spaces of appearance, the relations changes between the web and the space itself.

Therefore, the entirety of the web of relations and the entirety of all relationality between elements can never be 'seen' from an Archimedean point. It can never be fully charted or contained in any description. Only through its specific role, its particular manifestation, in a specific space of appearance, and in the construction of particular being-ness and meaning-in-common can humans sense the web and their sense of it is entirely through action within the space of appearance.

The web of relations as here conceived, therefore, attaches no pre-emptive or privileged value to one element within this web. Nor does it begin with a transfactual truth or law-producing mechanisms (Bhasker 1979, pp. 59–69.

It postulates a simple relationship in which the mechanism for the production of being-ness is established out of action, not thought. It ascribes no pre-emptive value to any aspect of the relation of action, social being-ness and meaning-in-common; nor to any aspect of the produced being-ness or meaning-in-common. What it seeks is simply to show the relation, constructed temporarily and mediated temporarily, between the various elements within any space of appearance.

Commonality dictates meaning and being-ness in a temporary form, a joint construction of particular action, the space of appearance, and the web of relations linked and acting together in a specific circumstance according to a specific configuration.

There are only instances of the particular; the general web can never be known. The web of relations is thus cross-hatched and displayed in many simultaneous forms; forms in which some relations are more complete, more multi-faceted and more developed than others.

Each aspect in which it presents itself is, in turn, entangled with other relational forms operating within the web. The totality of these relations is confirmed through the particular. What we mean here is the manner in which a local post office, for instance, confirms to us that there is a national postal network and therefore a national state. This is not a micro/macro instance because both macro and micro are contained within the same object, in this case the local post office. The creation of being-ness through actions of sociality is an ongoing, a dynamic, multi-stranded, multi-directional and infinite flow, akin to what Gergen terms the 'sea of supplementation' (1994, p. 31).

This step moves us away from the idealistic overstress on static meanings precisely because meaning in our account is constantly dependent upon relationality. As we established in Chapter 2, 'truth' is meaning held in common and is therefore subject to the same tentative status and temporality as the creation of being-ness.

Relations Between Meanings-in-Common, the Space of Relations and the Web of Relations

The web of relations is the inter-relation of all meanings-in-common expressed through actions of sociality. Action, affect and speech are always produced within the web because the web is the acts and words of human beings (Arendt op cit, p. 184; see also Gergen's notion of communal generation of meaning p. 31, 1994).

Let us use an example to unpack this difference between meanings-in-common and the web of relations.

Revisiting the Estate Office

In the office of the intervention anti-poverty programme on the estate, we discovered that there were deep, unspoken differences between the meanings-in-common held by various parties involved in the programme. These differences centred on particular meanings-in-common held by the estate residents and volunteers and the programme professionals.

These differences concerned, firstly, the terms under which the particular space of appearance, the community facility was to be used: for everyone? for the community? for the state-driven programme?

And, secondly, what form of being-ness was appropriate, and therefore allowed, inside the space/office. Could only the office manager give advice to clients? Should volunteers be consulted, not simply tasked?

While the volunteers, the Community Association and the paid professionals disagreed, often vehemently, sometimes to the point of leaving about variations of these two issues, nonetheless the vast majority remained within the meanings-in-common specific to the space.

That is, the volunteers deferred these differences and prioritised their common sense of what the programme meant for the estate. Despite differences, volunteers only complained about it to each other and performed the tasks they were given, so the office presented a steady front of help and assistance to the local people.

This all changed radically when the national funding came to an end and control of the office passed to a county-wide community umbrella body.

We argued earlier that the commonality creative of sustained meaning and being-ness are a specific outcome; that they change depending upon their relation to other elements.

In this case of the funding changes, a complex situation had arisen in which the funding of the office had changed hands and the parameters associated with that funding had changed with it. Thus, the commonality of ongoing meanings across the estate operated in changing circumstances in which the needs of the estate barely altered, but the terms under which the office was operated changed radically with the whims and concerns of new funders.

The volunteers felt no less outside when the new funders took over, but the latter found their insistence on the needs of the estate more troublesome. The new office funding has itself to be understood as being created within its own set of relations—devolved funding, local government and national government responsibility, third sector organisations, and so forth. It is when these two meet and overlap that we can begin to understand the complexity of the interlinking webs of relations and their production of meaning.

Following this change, it rapidly became apparent to the volunteers that they would not be able to pursue any element of their estate-derived agenda and so they left en masse, focussing instead on establishing other forms of community support, for example, starting a food kitchen, serving healthy and cheap cooked food for council workers and estate residents in the local leisure centre. In this way, they began to build and sustain their own meanings-in-common as an element within the entire town's web of relations.

What once had been a powerless, albeit majority, opinion within the previous anti-poverty programme, now gained greater stability as a meaning-held-in-common through the self-directed actions of the estate group. A stability enhanced by the materiality of both the kitchen and the weekly events. Thus, it began the process of creating its own presence in the wider web of relations through the increased circle of actions, and the increased repetition of particular being-ness creation.

This extension and development of Arendt's initial ideas therefore maintains the inter-relational, passive and active status of the web which functions in this sense, like plurality or any of the other elements initially included by Arendt in her account of human being-ness, Thinking about this inter-relationship, we also need to recall that being-ness once created, falls back into the wider web as another element, which in turn, conditions further action and being-ness creation.

Through these means, as outlined earlier, the inter-relationality of this analytic is established, and it is this inter-relationality which allows investigation into sociality somewhere to go.

What the analytic consists of therefore is an investigation of the terms of the temporary balance between the web and the space in any particular space of appearance; in other words, the particular terms operating for the creation of a social being-ness held in common.

The Web of Relations of the Moneyed Sector of Market-Town

We want to illustrate all of this with an analysis of the moneyed web of relations operating within Market-Town itself. We want to examine the terms for the creation of being-ness within its particular spaces of appearance. We will explore how this communal being-ness, created over time and lodged in the web of relations, impacts upon the town. What are its symbols and themes, its meanings-in-common? What are the barriers in which it contains itself, who does it include, and exclude; who are the powerless and who are the heard.

As we noted in Chap. 1, Market-Town sits within a county in which there are some of the wealthiest tax payers in this part of the UK. Its composition is much more varied, containing as many recently arrived settlers as it does generational inhabitants. This influx of retirees is very important to Market-Town, as it is to the entire county.

Amidst this however, as we have seen, the estate contains figures for poverty as debilitating as anywhere else in Britain: something concealed statistically by its surrounding areas of great wealth.

As one respondent stated,

Market Town is full of very rich people and very poor and there's not much in between.

What this section seeks to interrogate is the specific web of relations belonging and expressing the communal being-ness of the moneyed web, what we term the county set, in Market-Town.

We will examine linkages that provide the dynamic of the web as a force of both social power and communal being-ness within the town itself and its public life.

To do this requires a definition of social power, a definition which will be forthcoming from the evidence and case study presented.

At one end of the main street, a short distance from the Town Hall, sits the Towers Hotel. It is a tall, white, imposing Georgian building of three stories occupying the high corner of a strategic crossroads through town.

The Towers Hotel is the cornerstone, in many ways, of the moneyed county sector of Market-town and the surrounding county. It is the most frequent space of appearance for the sociality that actually sustains the web of relations of the 'county-set'. It is also a link in this web of relations.

An examination of the physicality of the Towers is a perfect site for the illustration of this particular web of relations: the web particular to wealthy Market-Town.

Outside the hotel, there are two large shiny copper pots with neat thin display trees much like there are in front of a rich London hotel, like the mythical Ritz. It is also the starting point for the annual Market-Town Boxing Day hunt, which has started here since the 1700's.

Here according to our field notes, most afternoons around 3.30, a Bentley or two discharges extremely well-dressed middle-aged women onto the pavement. They enter into the wide entrance foyer past the brass and polished wooden reception office, through the wide carpeted foyer; they move chatting through the granite-tiled courtyard past its display trees and neat table umbrellas, into the far reach of the Towers hotel past the second reception into the famous Towers tea room: a shaped tear-drop space with a bowled conservatory roof of glass, where waiters and waitresses in black uniforms and white aprons hurry between the tables.

The Towers afternoon tea, particularly its scones and cream, is famous in the county: 'it's the best afternoon tea in the county,' reported one interviewee.

There are 20–25 tables in this room and virtually every afternoon the room is full. The late afternoon flows around its glass ceiling and its expensive and manicured display vegetation. Hardly anyone sits alone. Businessmen, the occasional tourist, local solicitors, the even more infrequent older couple from the town, clearly distinguished by their diffident manner and lowly dress, all cross paths inside this tea room. Mostly, however, the crowd is women: very well-dressed middle-aged women, and very well-suited business types. Music plays discreetly but mostly the sound is the clinking of tea cups, the pouring of tea from sterling silver tea pots, and the low humming buzz of endless conversation.

So discreetly is all this routinely enacted, so removed is it from the rest of the life of the town, that the field notes record it was not until we had been in the town for 20 months that this space of appearance became visible to the eyes of the researchers.

Going back outside you walk, still on the ground floor, back down a carpeted corridor to the main public bar, which is quiet and kitted out in the style of a faux Victorian business class lounge. The usual signifiers: deep leather arm chairs; low glass-topped tables between leather couches; behind the bar the glass vase bigger than a bowl, stuffed with limes and the occasional lemon; the top shelf of malt whiskeys and the next shelf down, full of the most expensive brands of various spirits. None of them have a blue plastic tap at the bottom or bottles fixed upside down. There are no bar snacks but there are napkins with your drink and waiters who speak quietly and wait patiently. None of the waiting staff at the Towers are local, but have come in to work from across the EU, mostly France and Italy.

The Towers loves divided areas, and there is another one in the public bar; a discreet wide space spread at the back where soft leather sofas face each other across low, glass-topped tables.

From the public bar back out across the foyer, you pass quietly down some carpeted stairs to the basement. Through the floor-to-ceiling glass panelling at the foot of the stairs, you can see this room is kitted out like a gangster's boardroom in a crime movie: inset lights, polished leather wing-back chairs with curved raised sides, steel-coloured walls, inlaid lighting and in the middle a long polished oak table, larger than the entrance hallway in most British homes.

Back up the stairs, another set of wide stairs lead up to the second floor and the rooms. These rooms are expensive, far too expensive according to several scathing online reviews. Be what it may, that sort of hotel is not what the Towers is.

Crossing the outside courtyard again, under an arch, you come into the wide asphalt service area, extremely neat all the same, which runs between stables up a slight rise into the hotel's private car park, contained within old-fashioned stone-laid walls. Here sit a range of neatly parked, upmarket cars: Audis, BMWs, sporty-looking Range Rovers and the odd modern jag; several Audi TTs suggest the presence of land and property agents. Leave the car park past the patrons-only-sign, and you are back into the other Market-Town: the unemployed and aspirational Market-Town.

Returning down the slope towards the hotel buildings, you turn left and from the lobby in front of the tea room, you walk up some wide, beautifully carpeted stairs, sliding your palm up the deep polish of the oak bannister, stopping on the landing to admire the rising lead light window, finally reaching the Towers hotel ballroom on the first floor; which also has its own dedicated reception desk.

This is a real ballroom of the old Victorian type. The stage, tiny and almost useless, is far away, across a beautifully polished floor, beyond the huge chandelier which floats in the middle of the spreading space. It is the sort of floor where you want to take your shoes off and walk very quietly; after a while, you might even have a little slide in your socks.

Here, on an early weekday evening, once a month, meets the Market-Town Civic Society.

The Civic Society is a public forum for organised presentations and follow-up questions ostensibly concerning the town and its future. It hears about local initiatives of artistic, economic, historical or environmental relevance; county council plans things of this sort. Occasionally, they group together and spend some summer evening sweeping a small alley in the town or beautifying some long-standing area of litter, perhaps painting a little bit or erecting a bench. They have a monthly newsletter, emailed of course.

The meetings we attended contained approximately 50–60 people: predominately the well-heeled: older retirees, discreetly wealthy, country gentlemen and women, quietly secure financially, but also a smattering of prosperous-looking business people.

There are some upmarket artists; someone from the local history society and someone else who plays in a well-known jazz band. There is a reporter from the long-established local paper, people from the theatre, though no officials. Officials are rather lacking here; there is no-one from the town council, for instance, though upper echelon county council people are often present.

And around and through this crowd pass a regular parade of community consultants: those connected and those just 'finding their way'; every single one however displaying a uniform imperative to 'work the room'. One wonders if this is a scene repeated throughout the Market-Town ballrooms of the entire British Isles.

Studdert gave a presentation about our project, answered a few questions and asked a few questions during other presentations. One man spoke of a re-conservation programme taking place in the county: turning old factory wasteland back into green space. Someone from the county council gave an update on the long-term planning initiative for the county, and finally, a consultant from London gave a talk about the re-branding the town, citing examples of other towns who were 'ahead of the game' around Britain and stressing the need to be 'pro-active'.

Afterwards Studdert was approached by a local reporter and by a young woman inviting him to a meeting she was convening to discuss the formation of a tourist committee to present local businesses across Britain; a web site was mentioned.

When we think about this meeting, it is also interesting to reflect who wasn't there. There were no teachers from the under-performing secondary school, no councillors from the town council; no police or youth workers, no nurses; even the aspirational class was missing. It appears these groups know as little about the Towers Hotel web of relations as the Tower Hotel knows about them.

Ninety per cent of Market-Town appears to have very little awareness of this Towers hotel world. This unaware Market-Town, the Market-Town of the majority of people, moves about its own business, following its own tracks, shopping in its own shops. And the Towers hotel being-ness does the same.

The Saturday main street interviews, described in an earlier chapter, bear no trace of this Towers hotel world. Counting the vox pop interviews, we did over 200 interviews. It was mentioned once by an old couple from the estate when the husband said they had the best afternoon teas in the county. And this raises another point: for no one behaving properly ever appears to be refused entry into the Towers. No one interviewed openly confessed to feeling excluded. Yet no one mentioned it.

Indeed, a number of interviewees stated in relation to pubs that there were no barriers of class in any of the Market-Town pubs. It is simply that they never go to the Towers. On one occasion we invited some project participants to a meeting in the hotel. Two of them informed us that this was the first time they had been inside the Towers Hotel and were very excited. These two people came from the estate and clearly the hotel had a role in their fantasy life, that is, it related to their meanings-in-common concerning the town. Yet they had never been there.

You can see the traces of the hotel's presence by simply standing outside it any day of the week. The shop next door is an expensive, very upmarket florist. Next to that is another extremely expensive real estate agent. On the opposite corner is an expensive jeweller. Twenty yards away are two very discreet upmarket women's boutiques both with severe modernist window displays. Another 20 yards will take you to the front door of the town hall. The fact these shops and buildings are primarily clustered within close walking distance of the Towers hotel seems unlikely to be accidental.

The county-set web of relations discreetly circulates throughout the town; through the shops mentioned earlier, through the high-end delicatessen; the top end real estate agents, the expensive arts and craft shop next to the upmarket food and trifles store, through Bunts, the upmarket everything-store discreetly set back behind columns 40 yards from Tesco's, which features, at the back, another upmarket tea room which the Towers ladies often frequent in the morning.

Yet these sites, and the web of relations which they sustain, are distinguished as much by absence as by presence. As we noted, they barely featured in our interviews, nor do our field notes record much discussion about them.

Since, generally speaking, the Towers Hotel crowd did not live in the town or join the crowds in the mall on a Saturday morning, we, in common with other social scientists (Savage), found it almost impossible to gain access to or interview these people.

So this web of relations circulates within groups, habits, locations within the town rather than the town itself.

This is a web of relations further sustained and enhanced by other similar social groupings: the history society, the tennis club, various community forums, the business club and the Masons. These groupings in the main are composed of strands of similar people, apparently all known to each other. It is sustained by repetitive social inter-relations productive of recognisable being-ness and meanings-in-common.

The moneyed web is constituted through communal meanings which imply, among other things, authority, ownership and correct ways of being. When we embarked on the historical strand of our project to bridge divisions within Market-Town, we held an initial meeting above a pub in the centre of town: 'The Bent Shovel'. Our initial meeting was attended by two people from the Civic Society. They mentioned other historical societies in the town and when asked if they were interested in working with our developing group, they simply replied, 'no, we're only here to observe.' They also attended other functions we held, once again they sat by themselves offering no input, but simply 'observing'. We could understand this observation as an action creative of meanings about the right kind of knowledge and way of doing things. Yet it is not governance, it is entirely informal, a communal being-ness which calls forth this obligation to attend.

This right way of doing things and ownership of meaning was further exemplified by a contestation over the meaning of local history.

As reported to us in a formal interview, one young professional, having recently re-located to Market-Town, sought to attend the local history society meetings, to learn more about the town, as she said, and because she was interested in history.

I did try and join the local history society last year um and because of dealing with the children I think I turned up maybe 10 minutes into and I was glared at when I walked through the door because it was already sort of under way and at the end I hung I was approaching groups of people but they really did seem quite reluctant to let me in, which is understandable cause it's probably been the same people for years. It just seemed a quite cliquey environment.

Shortly after our initial meeting at the Bent Shovel, we received, out of the blue, a letter from a person involved in various history projects around the town. The letter was written by someone who had read about the Forgotten Market-Town Facebook page in the local paper. The writer, who seemed somewhat incensed that s/he had not previously heard of this, went on to enquire in a somewhat aggressive tone, what local history projects had been carried out locally and implied that, as project researchers, we clearly knew nothing about genuine local history. S/he ended by demanding to know when the next meeting of this so-called history group was taking place.

What comes through very strongly is the sense of ownership of the town's history and the author's general tone of surprise at our presumption.

Other groupings within the town perform a similar discreet screening role. In our interviews, we asked three current or recent female town councillors and two current male councillors: do the Freemasons run Market-Town? All three women laughed and responded in the affirmative; both men looked worried and surprised and answered in the negative. One former county council employee recalled in an interview how, as recently as the 1990s, application forms for jobs with the county council, routinely contained as one of the written questions, the following sentence: *are you a member of any community self-help groups, for example, the Masons?*

Finally, before we begin our analysis of all this information, we want to discuss one more element.

The local Market-Town paper announced one day that major royalty will visit a local business in Market-Town in the next few days.

Royal visits are not uncommon in Market-Town; this was the third since we'd started the project. What is interesting is that in our two years in the town interviewing over 200 people, attending meetings in all parts of town and with all sorts of people, we had barely heard mention of this company. It operates so it seems, on a different radar to other firms and other parts of the town. Indeed, the article informs us that

> *The business…, has a host of celebrity and international royalty among its clientele.*

And further that the majority of its business is one line, with customers spending £1000s simply based on the company's reputation for production and service.

We have heard much in our interviews concerning factories which closed in the 1980s, leaving the town devoid of employment opportunities. However, online companies of the sort mentioned here, even one who serves clients like Hollywood film stars and royalty, have never rated a mention in any interview.

How Do We Study This Web?

Many sociologists have complained about the difficulty of sociological research on the lives of the contemporary rich (Savage and Williams 2008). It is certainly true that studies of the working class under various guises, far outnumber accounts of the social world of the rich and powerful.

Using this simple analytical coupling of the space of appearance and the web of relations, we will describe and analyse the moneyed web of relations within Market-Town. We will theorize it as a 'who' constructive of being-ness, incorporating materiality, subjectivity; constructive of meanings in common and through those meanings more action in public, more sociality and more being-ness in common.

Along the way, we will examine how these communal meanings play out in the town, how they impact generally on the town itself, and, specifically, how they impact on divisions within the town.

In terms of the thread of this monograph, we want to move beyond the space of appearance, to the wider effect, in terms of social being-ness, of actions contained within the moneyed web of relations.

In terms of our mode of investigation, we want to examine social being-ness within a sub-community of the town, discovering how they maintain their particular social cohesion and how this social cohesion plays out in all facets of the town's ongoing communal being-ness.

Let Us Begin by Asking the Following Questions

What are the terms productive of this moneyed being-ness? Where does it occur? How does it link into a web of relations? Let's think about what is being created in the long-standing space of appearance within the Towers hotel.

We can start with the people who attend. This afternoon tea is a ritual of sociality. It exists as means of linking and activating relations and meanings within the moneyed web of relations. It is a space where the moneyed group appear to themselves, as they appear to their peers. The presence of tourists or the odd visitor from the estate sampling 'the best afternoon tea in the county', is not a hindrance to this action of appearance, they are simply ignored. They play no part in the creation of a specific being-ness, nor in the creation of the meanings-in-common attached to that being-ness.

These are all people who appear similar; similar, but not entirely the same. Of course they all see the world slightly differently, they all have varying interests and to that extent there is a limited degree of plurality within these spaces of appearance: the Civic Society and the hotel. Moreover, this limited plurality and difference is one element sustaining of their own image of themselves, as it is also sustaining of the possibilities for the creation of being-ness required in the space. Yet they also share certain commonalities of dress; they live, commonly, in the county, rather than the town. They have friends in the room or acquaintances of long standing. They all exhibit, almost as if it provides ontological security, the symbolic artillery of wealth, even if they are faking it.

They speak in very similar tones; they greet and meet in a familiar and practised way. Their manners, their modes of interaction, their dress, their watches, their cars, all these link them together as parties similar and recognisable to each other. And of course, these two things, their plurality and their similarity, are both elements in shaping their social being-ness. The one they hold in common.

This eternal re-production of a certain being-ness also imbues the physical structure of the Towers hotel.

The hotel is a sedimented collection of meanings-in-common within the web of relations, one which activates relations and linkages. The Civic Society is simply an acknowledgement and an extension of this informal tea-room sociality.

Presence at these meetings indicates not just an assumed 'responsibility for the town's well-being' but also signals an awareness of this role; in turn, the responsible assumption of this role serves to justify the tea room and the hotel. It allows every anointed space (and that being-ness that emerges from those spaces) to be verified, recognised and vindicated.

At the same time, this contemporary moneyed web of relations is not available as a space open to the wider public. This production of being-ness does not take place in a public town hall before the entire town; or any other common public space in which a different plurality of views could circulate, a space where, for instance, the estate's view can be heard as equals.

Rather the being-ness is created in the sociality particular to that sort of space. It is discreet and recessed, set back and held in the Towers hotel ballroom, and afterwards, having a quick drink in the bar.

It exists in a limited, self-contained and commonly constructed series of spaces of appearance: the Towers tea room, the Civic Society meetings, the various shops, business, groups and forums, online and off-line worlds mentioned earlier.

One result of this situation is that this being-ness can only be seen by the rest of the town, through 'tears in the curtain' or when the moneyed communal being-ness chooses to display itself, for example, at the annual festival which we will discuss later.

How it can be seen however, is through the traces present in its own construction of being-ness and meaning-in-common. These traces are in fact the linking devices embedded into communal being-ness, in the extended web and also present within the space of appearance itself.

So the themes and meanings which mark any single space of appearance fall back into and run through all future sociality and hence the future construction of being-ness through action and containment.

One example of this is the blurring of boundaries. This is a theme running through many spaces of appearance; this is a common thread running through the administration of Market-Town; it runs through the very status of the hotel which contains both the tea room and the Civic Society. Boundaries are blurred between the town and county councils in regard to responsibilities and in the material control of town resources. It is blurred between the county council: its specific area committee, and the town council. It is blurred by the presence on the town council of councillors who are both town councillors and county councillors. It is blurred in the status of the festival: is it private or public? It is blurred in the account of the royal visit: was it a visit to the town or to this particular business?

This blurring is also present in the space of appearance: the meeting of the Civic Society itself. For what is the status of this meeting? Is it a public event or a private one? Is it a town, or a county group?

In the recently published plan for the town and surrounding areas, the county council wrote the following.

Town centre partnership—Bringing together the various interests around a shared forum for promoting collective and individual action on town centre issues. This 'Town Team' should consist of representatives of

- *County Council*
- *Town Council*
- *Business Club*
- *Market Traders*
- *The Rotary Club*
- *Independent businesses*
- *Interested community groups e.g. Civic Society*

Given that it is the only community group listed as a consultative partner by the county council, what is its status? Does it speak for the community? Are the people attending concerned citizens or business people with specific interests? Many people are joint members of all these bodies.

Furthermore, aside from the market traders, everyone else mentioned in that list comes from the same milieu: the Rotary club, the Business club, independent businesses, these are simply different names for what amounts to a monolithic business interest. Where are the residents' forums, the sporting clubs or the voluntary societies which dot the town? This is a very limited palate of the town's ongoing activity.

Such a blurring of boundaries, in which one interest is represented by different titles, is maintained and validated through the ongoing creation of being-ness within the Civic Society itself. There is a two-way flow between the Civic Society space and this web of relations.

Another element present within the creation of being-ness within the space of appearance is the practice of discreetness; a setting back amounting almost to withdrawal from the social world of the entire town. This is exhibited in the space of appearance by the hotel's hiring of waiting staff exclusively from Europe. It is exhibited by the simple fact that no one from, for example, the estate, has ever, as far as we know, spoken or addressed a Civic Society meeting.

All of this constructs from its repetitive action and containment, the terms of the creation of being-ness within the Civic Society, back and forth from sociality through the wider web of relations.

This elusiveness, this withdrawal, this exclusivity, is indicated not just by the choice of topics for discussion, but also in the practices of wider organisations linked into the space of appearance of the Civic Society. For instance, the theme of exclusivity, present in the ballroom, mirrors and reinforces the tendency towards secrecy and discreetness of operation in other voluntary groups linked into the moneyed web of relations. We have seen the history society and its sense of exclusiveness. The answers provided to our questions concerning the Masons illustrate this secrecy as well. The male interviewees, whether or not they themselves were Freemasons, clearly did not feel comfortable with the subject, a stance which acknowledges both its mystification and its influence. While the women, who are of course excluded from meetings and the Freemasons, simply responded in a manner which revealed that they too shared the general suspicions, characteristic of most of the town.

What these two examples show is how the action of sociality travels back and forth along between the space of appearance and the web of relations.

And what the sum total of all the actions of sociality reveals is the communal being-ness: a communal being-ness held in common ('a community') and expressed through action and materiality by the moneyed county set of Market-Town.

The Moneyed Expression of Communal Being-ness

Having established how the moneyed web of relations creates and sustains itself through sociality, let us examine the character of this moneyed web of relations: the themes and symbols expressive of its sense of itself-its communal being-ness.

Let's begin by looking at the projects discussed in the meetings of the Civic Society we attended. We described how the audience listened to people outlining various projects of civic significance. How at the end of each 20 minutes presentation, the seated audience engaged in lively questioning.

For all of this, however, there is a strange abstraction about these civic improvement projects. They do not include projects to improve the standard of the lowly rated Town high school, for instance, or proposals to fund a badly needed GP for the estate, or ideas on how to help people with specific problems, for example, disabled children.

Rather, these projects are of a certain type, noticeably more directed to the county than the town: well-intentioned plans to provide more green space through re-generation projects, gloomy futuristic projections concerning the economic future of the county delivered by the deputy head of the county council. Finally, there is a consultant from outside the county, who presents the town to the audience as a supine object, an abstraction requiring constant branding and re-branding to attract tourists. This is followed by further questions, announcements, opportunities for consultation and drinks. As we observed this, we were struck by the lack of presence within this evening of the town itself. It seemed that the interests of the county filled up the space.[3]

So if the town is absent from the communal being-ness of the Market-Town Civic Society, what is there in its place? What is the picture of the town which the Towers hotel pronounces as its meanings-in-common, its communal being-ness?

An example that might help answer this question is the Market-Town annual festival.

This festival is known all over the country. Its overall running is contracted to a private firm. As far as we know it is not put out to public tender by the council, and the council, beyond supplying the market hall, has no role in running the festival. Roads are closed and traffic is diverted.

What the festival reveals is the moneyed web of relation's idea of its own communal being-ness. It is here that the being-ness created through the tea room, the Civic Society, and all the rest asserts itself as communal meaning and social power, a step which furthers the ongoing construction of being-ness in common, produces further meanings-in-common, and sediments and reinforces the communal being-ness expressed through it as an event.

It is here that these spaces of appearance express themselves as coherent social power constructed by communal meanings and persistent sociality. It is a Towers hotel version of Market-Town, and its own communal being-ness as a force in Market-Town.

It is also a space of appearance constructed to exclude as much as it includes.

There are lots of details around the festival which support this last claim. Firstly, the festival has an entrance fee, a fee for entry into what is, usually free public space. The hall is jammed with people and business displays; indeed, the festival runs over into nearby buildings and via closed-off streets outside, into the wider town. Inside the market hall, the

---

[3] Indeed, since this passage was written, we have had an opportunity to observe the notice board erected in the main shopping precinct by the Market-Town Civic society. This lists the Civic Society's current two projects in relation to the town as (1) discussing with the council the 'my place town future plan' and (2) discussion of a colour palette for the main street. In neither instance was consultation from the town invited. The activities were simply presented as a statement of fact.

displays are expensive conceptions. There are lots of clean canvas and displays decked in apparel and bunting. Crowds are huge though many simply stare and appear nervous sampling the wares. There are lots of quaint uniforms on those people running the stalls. Red is the primary colour. As reported by respondent H1, these people tempting you with their thousand different flavours are predominately in their 20s or younger. They are blonde tanned and mostly over six feet. They are dressed in chinos, that casual ironed and spotless way which denotes money: chinos, white shirts and waist coats.

They look richer than their customers.

Craft is the overriding theme. The stress is on 'individuality', 'uniqueness', 'particularity', 'purity', 'exclusiveness'. Old themes dressed in new language: 'localism', 'organic', 'hand-made', 'history', 'online' and 'craft'.

There are specialist products from every grid reference on the ordinance map. Indeed any sort of comprehensive description of the goods on offer cannot help but sound like one of Rimbaud's Illuminations.

For most of Market-Town, the festival is a fairyland.

There are a lot of these sorts of fairy lands in the modern world: the Olympic village is another; constructed on a similar but much larger sense of elite communal being-ness; imbued with the same qualities, on a vast social scale (Broudehoux, Anne-Marie in David and Monk 2007).

The festival is where the communal being-ness of the moneyed web of relations in Market-Town can be seen; its meanings-in-common dominate the space of appearance.

All of this shows a certain reflexivity by the county set concerning its own place, its own role, about how to maintain this role, the terms indeed through which it interacts with the town outside of the Tower Hotel, outside their own web of moneyed relations. This communal being-ness displays certain themes; symbols and practices which reflect its communal being-ness to the public and just as important, to itself.

The online world is drenched with glamour, royalty and Hollywood. It is presented that way in the local newspaper: as a glamorous picture of itself which everyone can share.

All of this has the hallmark of a developed and sophisticated web of relations fully self-aware and acting out a shared meaning-in-common concerning its own communal being-ness. The two members from the Civic Society, who attended our meeting, are also suggestive of this sort of communal reflexivity. They could have appeared in the 'Bent Shovel' in any number of roles: local historians; members of the town; punters, or what they were, members of the Civic Society. They chose to describe themselves as 'just interested bystanders' who 'probably wouldn't come to another meeting' and as members of the Civic Society. All of this suggests, in a social form, the communal being-ness that the Civic Society and the moneyed web of relations acts/speaks and appears from. It shows a need to maintain its role, to define and understand other alternative meanings-in-common circulating throughout the town.

This is true also of the letter from the woman connected with the history society, with its attempt to dispute and undermine any other versions of history or grouping, its tone of social approval given and withheld. The closed ranks towards newcomers, indeed the coherent construction of their own spaces of appearance where all elements from sociality to meanings-in-common to web of relations can be invoked, and involved in the creation of more communal being-ness, speaks of the same reflexivity and understanding of itself as communal being-ness.

So the county set in Market-Town produces, through an integrated web of relations, the communal being-ness they wish to present to the town, as well as a reflexivity concerning its existence as communal being-ness within the town. It is a communal being-ness grounded in the sociality, within the walls of the Towers Hotel.

The Running of Market-Town

This 'setting-back', this slow retreat of the moneyed web from the social world in public, could be understood as an act of communal being-ness and communal meaning. It is an acting in concert, visible all through this particular web of relations. The withdrawal has many facets. It is manifest in the types of people within the hotel's various spaces of appearance. It is symbolised by the hotel's unwillingness to employ anyone with a local accent and by the concentration of the county set, not on the people in the town they ostensibly claim to speak for, but rather on those it can *attract* to the town.

However, this withdrawal from large portions of the public life of Market-Town does not stop the Civic Society from being the only representative voice cited when the town council released their recent local consultation procedures for future town planning, as we have seen.

This withdrawal from the social life of the town, the severing of links of employment and presence, has however had no effect upon the communal being-ness, the social power of the moneyed web to exert their perspective as dominant through the town council and into the county administration. Moreover, it exerts its communal being-ness in ways that the majority of town folk we interviewed viewed as having been detrimental to the town for a long time.

As we noted at the outset much of this moneyed web lives, not in the town itself, but in the surrounding countryside.

In every major battle between town and county council, the county wins at the expense of the town. The history of the open-air pool illustrates that.

Exactly the same style of transfer occurred, concerning the recent 'returning' of the children's park to town control. Just as in the pool case no compensating financial aid was offered by the county to help in maintain the facility after it was 'returned'.

As we saw many people blamed the council for the deterioration of the town. However when asked, many also had trouble separating decisions made by the town council, from those enacted by the county council. This blurring of boundaries allows the perspective of the moneyed communal being-ness to pass back to town the upkeep of expensive public facilities of any sort, not used by the moneyed communal being-ness. The return of the skate park represents a classic example of this process by which the town council in its own name is made responsible for expensive county public responsibilities which can, with no financial assistance in the future, only deteriorate until they are closed. Meanwhile, it distracts the town council from using money for schemes within the town by tying up town council money.

This diminishing of the town council as an office for the benefit of the entire town, is often traced back to the local government act of 1982 which stripped power from town councils and re-located it in the hands of the county. Whatever the consequences of that act, the diminishing positioning of the Market-Town council as a source of authority within the town is further confirmed by the simple fact that town councillors are also simultaneously members of the county council.[4] As we recorded in our field notes, we were told that the minority usually bowed to the superior knowledge of majority. The result is that the interest of the town gets lost and decisions made at county level are simply ratified whatever their particular consequences for the town.

However, this diminishing of the town council accords with the county-based perspective exhibited in the Towers hotel ballroom meeting of the civic society. It existed in the topics discussed, the topics deemed of interest.

This subservience of the town council deprives the town of an independent voice, a voice speaking in the town's own interest and it replaces it with a county-friendly view that simply ignores the voice of the town and confines its town council activities to painting the store facades in the main street.

This is further supported by the reasoning attendant upon council decisions. In our discussion of the pool in Chapter 4, we described the common terms the town councillors used in describing the process and thinking behind its closure, as constituting a meaning-in-common. This is a meaning-in-common, one expressed in managerial and finance terms, which ignored the wishes of the population to keep it open. By relying on a financial argument and one that saw equivalence between an open-air pool and a leisure centre, the council failed to engage in any creative or collaborative discussion about the decision to be taken.

Thus the moneyed web of relations expresses its meanings-in-common, its communal being-ness, as social power; a social power which

---

[4] This is a very high proportion for the county as a whole. In a rich village/town 20 minutes away from Market-Town, the town council only has one member out of nine who is simultaneously a member of both. It is notable in this village that the town council is more active in the town's interests.

defines the town council's role to itself, that makes it enunciate as its own, a perspective which surrenders power to the county.

Social power therefore becomes the self-conscious and specific acting out of meanings-in-common by particular groupings to one degree of effect or another.

Creating and Sustaining of Divisions Within the Town

The contemporary web of relations of the Market-Town's moneyed and powerful is intentionally set back from the town's public immediate life and it is done so as an action of communal being-ness.

The activities and being-ness surrounding the Towers hotel are largely unknown to the estate; but they are also just as unknown to the aspirational middle class of Market-Town. However, as we have seen, the moneyed communal being-ness presents a view of the town to the town, through a wide range of activities including a royal visit and the festival.

In our interviews many Market-Town people mentioned the festival. Many expressed a desire to attend, but very few of them did so, simply because most of them could not afford to.

This event as much as it serves to highlight the 'success' on the town's intention to attract tourism, also marks the new limit on what the moneyed web of relations regards as the town. It excludes even as it exudes.

Anyone attending the usual weekly market, say on Monday, Thursday or Friday would immediately notice a sizeable difference between that market and the festival: routinely the town market on these days consists of vast unused spaces with rows of bare tables; reduced numbers of outlets; meat-freezer temperatures in the winter; bored traders talking to each and the occasional shopper.

It is highly debatable whether the festival contributes anything to this version of Market-Town. What is does serve very efficiently is a web of moneyed relations spreading out, first through the county and then wider, through the counties beyond. Of course, it also precisely brands the town as a scenic place to visit, which is home to excellent products for the discerning shopper, precisely the target audience for the county set and the town council.

That this perspective entirely informs the town council perspective became clear to us when we commissioned some young people to write and perform a piece at the local theatre. The piece was brilliantly executed and centred on complaints about drugs, bullying and having nothing to do. At the interval we were approached by one town councillor who strongly objected to this portrayal of the town, because 'it gave a bad image of Market-Town to outsiders'. Conversely, he was utterly uninterested in the issue raised by these young people of Market-Town, issues so clearly and movingly portrayed in the piece.

Meanwhile, up on the estate, they can't find work, and the sort of business activity favoured by the moneyed web of relations is unlikely to ever provide it. Recent suggestions that development applications for a new supermarket should be approved only if it was accompanied by agreements ensuring the employment of a certain percentage of local people, were simply brushed aside by the town and county councils as impossible under health and safety legislation.

Here again, the moneyed web of relations with their county perspective prevails over the requirements of the town for jobs to maintain their communal stability.

It is one of the telling ironies of the changes we describe, that historically when the poor of the town refused to work they were locked inside the workhouse; now when they want to work, they are excluded from the upmarket businesses, housed in the restored tourist-orientated workhouse.

The policy of exclusion illustrated by this example is deep-seated and well engrained in every aspect of the town's life from the economic to the spatial.

There is one bus stop in Market-Town's main street. It is not outside the Towers hotel. It is at the other end, at the bottom, opposite Tesco's. Here, just as they do at the nearby cab rank, people queue day and night taking their shopping back home up the hill.

Meanwhile, through the pedestrian mall and out the other side, just over a different hill, just down from the town hall, well-heeled patrons enter into the hallows of the Towers hotel.

This simple juxtaposition marks the divisions in Market-Town: divisions of power, emanating from communal being-ness and created in sociality.

Space and Geography

The Civic Society is called the Market-Town Civic Society.

But at its heart, in the geographical centre of this web, instead of Market-Town itself, there is a bare hole of empty vacated space where the town council should be, but isn't. And this bare hole sits cheek by jowl with a recessed, moneyed web of relations, recreating through sociality their communal being-ness, inside the Towers hotel.

This created division, this created absence, separating the county moneyed set from the town it purports to exist in and serve, this withdrawal process which marks the sociality of this contemporary moneyed web of relations, takes place in spaces and geographies far removed from those operating in pre-1960s period.

In the late 1950s, the working class lived in the middle of Market-Town as they had for hundreds of years, in streets centred round Henry St. This overall area of three to five streets was packed with tenements and people. Henry Street not only placed the poor in the centre of town, it meant that their presence had to be contested in public. The main streets of the town, the town hall and the market hall couldn't be left to Henry Street. Policing was active, jailing was frequent. Henry Street demanded a countervailing presence as a form of containment by the moneyed town upon the town. It forced the moneyed groupings to appear in public. After the war, the presence and communal being-ness of Henry Street and the Market-Town working poor was further asserted through the factories which ringed the town and employed numbers into their hundreds.

In this old Tory, One Nation, Market-Town, the poor, the working class, the middle class and the rich constantly engaged with each other, albeit in positions of dependency and superiority. Many of the people at the Towers tea room came from families which 60 years before would have lived in houses that employed people downstairs from Henry Street, people who were active participants in, and lived alongside the very rich in almost every aspect of their lives.

The father of CT1, whom we shall meet again in Chap. 7, was a chauffeur for a lord who lived just outside the town. Another interviewee worked during the early 1960s first in the kitchen of the Towers and then as a hotel maid.

At that time the enactment of privilege in that Market-Town, was in many ways a much more public affair, enacted in public, creating for both groups, a series of particular meanings-in-common that sustained, even in its opposition, some sort of common communal being-ness. This real plurality of different views uttered in public and contested in public has now, to all intents and purposes, entirely disappeared from Market-Town.

This pre-1960s Britain with its stifling formality, its habit of people being addressed by surnames, its dress codes being acted out in public and its hierarchy also being acted out within constant public spaces of appearance, meant that the edifice of class was apparent to all elements within the town, as it was throughout the country.

Now these factories are gone and the people from Henry Street have been re-located to the windy hill on the outskirts of the town.

The effect of this change to space and geography is a huge vacuum at the centre of the social world of Market-Town. A vacuum created firstly, by the re-location of families and neighbours from Henry Street to the estate, and secondly, by the simultaneous, or shortly thereafter, renunciation by the Civic Society and the moneyed web of relations from much of their previous public involvement in the public life of the town. These closely conjunct withdrawals have left the physical town to decline, becoming in the process more divided and more entrenched in its class difference and inequality.

Bibliography

Arendt, H. (1958). *The human condition*. Chicago: University of Chicago Press.
Bhaskar, R. A. (1989). *Reclaiming reality: A critical introduction to contemporary philosophy*. London: Verso.

David, M., & Monk, D. B. (2007). *Dream worlds of neoliberalism: Evil paradises.* New York: The New Press.

Gergen, K. (1994, May). Exploring the postmodern: Perils or potentials? *American Psychologist, 49*(5), 412–416.

Rorty, R. (1989). *Contingency, irony & solidarity.* New York: Cambridge University Press.

Rose, N. (1999). *Powers of freedom.* Cambridge: Cambridge University Press.

Savage, M., & Williams, K. (2008). *Remembering elites* (The sociological review). Malden, MA: Blackwell.

Studdert, D. (2006). *Conceptualising community: Beyond the state and the individual.* London: Palgrave.

6

Space, Geography and Social Power

Oh Henry Street, I wish they had never pulled it down. But they pulled it down, the council, and now it is nothing, the police station is built there, the job centre is put there, nothing.

Do you remember a time when Market-Town was much more prosperous? Oh yeah.

Chapter 5 sought to show the linkage, the meanings-in-common, between the county set and the council. The bulk of this chapter will be devoted to an examination of the other end of Market-Town: the meanings-in-common of working Market-Town.

This will begin with an examination of the communal being-ness of Henry Street. Historically, the centre of the slum streets of Market-Town, Henry Street existed in the middle of the town until the 1950s when the inhabitants were moved to an estate on the town's northern outskirts.

Henry Street ran parallel to the main shopping street. It lay closer to the river and historically had often been flooded.

The mention of this street, like the mention of the open-air swimming pool, elicited strong reactions from people: gleeful outbursts and arm

© The Author(s) 2016
D. Studdert, V. Walkerdine, *Rethinking Community Research*,
DOI 10.1057/978-1-137-51453-0_6

waving. Whenever it was raised in interviews, meetings or conversation, it invariably elicited stories which were often elaborated by others. There was a commonality about the telling and about the meanings. As one respondent remarked, its influence was felt throughout the whole town.

Another thing the interviews revealed was that Henry St is only the narrative centre, the signifier for these meanings-in-common; in fact, these memories encompass far more than simply one street. They include the entire working life of the town, actioned through railways, pubs, factories, public space, socialities, communal life, and modes and places of entertainment.

In short, it evokes a communal being-ness and its accompanying web of relations.

Of course, many of the 'props' sustaining of this particular web of relations have disappeared. This disappearance was a slow process, stretching from the early 1960s to the end of the 1980s.

That is the world Henry Street evokes—the world as it was prior to out-of-town supermarkets, online shopping, motorways, town council 'reforms', railway closures, globalisation, the closure of factories, slum clearance, town planning, community policing, dead-beat-dads, both parents working, and all the rest.

We do not propose to study this actual lost world in any sort of specific detail or historical depth. Henry Street and the rest of that world—the railway terraces, the trains and bridges, the factories and mines—these are things that sat in that world within their own multi-stranded web of relations. They served the same function of balancing its web of relations as does the Towers Hotel. It was a world where physical objects, social power, factories, unions and grinding poverty were an everyday reality, creative of a constant sociality and a constant communal being-ness. One in which communal meanings-in-common were expressed continually through sociality and the endless construction of being-ness held in common.

That world has disappeared.

All that is left are the meanings-in-common and their presence in current communal being-ness and that is what we propose to study: Henry St as a contemporary meaning-in-common, the survival of the sociality, and being-ness sourced in the habits, memories and sociality of that world and remaining in contemporary Market-Town.

It is also a meaning-in-common held by people, who, to some degree or other, feel excluded from modern Market-Town.

We want to examine what effects this exclusion has had upon the present world of the town. We want to interrogate how this loss is understood and maintained against the alternative 'being-ness account' offered by the county set. In short, we want to examine the present state of this meaning-in-common in relation to its contemporary social space and communal geography.

Henry Street: What Is Its Meaning in Common?

We have previously mentioned the Facebook page that we created to explore popular local history and memories as part of one of our projects. This chapter will use comments from that page and from oral history interviews conducted in a local hall. It also draws on data from the narrative, vox pop and focus group interviews.

The first quote will set the scene describing what Henry Street was like in this period prior to its demise. It comes from a participant who grew up there and was part of the later move to the estate. This first quote is intended to describe the many aspects of the street.

If I say what my impressions of Henry Street were: I always knew from when I was small that it was probably the roughest, toughest street in Town. But the sense of community was absolutely unbelievable. Basically nobody had anything. If you had nothing you'd get half off somebody else. And also there was a big sense of natural justice, a wonderful sense. I can remember my grandmother saying if you clipped a child around the ear for nothing, you'd get one back. And it was that sort of street that everybody looked after everybody else.

And what happened if you clipped them around the ear for something?

Oh, that was fine, that was fine. Maybe it was their law, maybe it was Henry Street law, I don't know.

And who, as it were, kind of policed that?

The oldest families in Market-Town. There were a lot of old families in Market-town—still is—and to me they still hold sway because there's a lot goes on underneath. People don't realise that the old families have held sway for many, many years.

Was it just a kind of social influence or was it like did they have any money or…?

No, very few had money on Henry Street. There were one or two people who had money but it wasn't flashed about as it is now, to say "Oh, look what I've got". Because most people didn't have anything in those days. I know because I didn't realise it till I grew up that because we always had pheasant on the table, salmon, trout, I didn't realise my father was poaching. I didn't know. It was normal food. It was rabbits.

Where was he poaching it?

All around. By the river and everywhere else he'd go, you know.

Who owned all that land?

Anybody and everybody. If he thought he could get something for dinner he'd go and get it.

And where did people work at that time?

Well my father worked on the Borough Council. The railways were big then. There was building merchants. There was a wood-yard on Henry Street. There was also a rag stores on Henry Street.

Ah okay, so there was quite a lot of things actually on Henry Street.

Yeah, actually on Henry Street, besides the rest of the town.

So there was a kind of sense in which, for some people, you never had to leave Henry Street.

Exactly, because there was plenty of shops and whatever.

And the houses, what sort of houses were they?

Well people say to me it was all slums but it wasn't because there was some really nice houses there that actually could've been left alone and done up. I'm not saying some of the housing wasn't bad because there was what you call courts. You went through a passageway and there were little houses at the back of other houses, and some of those had dirt floors. And some of those were not so good. The house we lived in was a four-storey town house, which is what they're building now. That's where the Henry thing came from because it was actually started in Henry's Tudor times; it's the oldest street in Market-Town.

And those places tend to really encourage a kind of communal... because everyone can see everybody else and they all mix at the bottom, and the kids play at the bottom and the kids can watch them and it's kind of all cut off from the street.

This is what I'm saying: the community was there, all the way down the street.

But it's a kind of product of the architecture too, isn't it?

Yes, that helped. And the fact that there were a lot of families lived in the street. My father was one of twelve children and they were, my grandmother and grandfather lived in the street - my paternal grandmother and grandfather - and I think there were seven other children lived in the street. And at home so there was nine out of the twelve of them lived on that street. Eventually some of them moved away when they started knocking down bits.

And how tall were the houses? Were they flats that people lived in or did they live in the whole house?

They used to live in rooms, didn't they. They didn't live in flats then, did they? You'd get like rooms; two rooms or whatever.

Ah right. And in those two rooms the kids all slept in one room?

Possibly. I mean I don't remember because we always lived in the house but my mother's mother lived there, my mother and father, my sister and her husband and the five brothers. There were thirteen of us at one time. Now it would considered over-crowded. But all I know is that there was always somebody there to play with; there was always somebody there.

We understand from this that Henry Street presented a very clear space of its own, in which communality and caring for one another were very strong components. This is echoed by others. For example:

Everybody dug their gardens and you shared the stuff. In a block of four, we was, in Henry Street. We all had a garden but we were so close, one would grow potatoes, the other cabbage and sprouts and everything would be shared out and given to people who didn't have a lot of stuff. Nothing was wasted. There was more community spirit, as much as there's community spirit now there was more then than there ever is today.

As someone else adds:

You always felt safe. Always safe because there was always family there. Yes, there was always someone around.

The safety aspect is developed by this participant who describes her husband's sentiment towards Henry Street:

Oh my husband was born in Henry Street. He always says it was a lovely place with beautiful buildings. He gets really cross when they call it 'slums'.

Many other participants echo these sentiments, discussing the poaching, along with the sense of plenty generated by beer and ice-cream produced locally; others speak of the lines of older women who having finished their housework stood outside chatting and 'watching over' the street.

Henry Street and the Rest of Market-Town

Of course, Henry Street in these discussions is also a signifier for a wider view of the town in that period. Although there are gradations and differences, what comes across strongest is a sense of a vital communal being-ness inhabiting the centre of the town, and it is this that contrasts so markedly with the same town space described in the previous chapter.

This contrast is presented pointedly by a participant who remembers it from a child's perspective:

Oh my golly. It was unbelievable. You know, you'd have twenty, thirty, forty trains there. There was the head driver. There was Mr Albert Harper. But you'd see men going down there, they were called firemen, because their job was to light the fire and get the water up. What we used to like doing was going down there and they'd cook their breakfast on a shovel in the fire, black pudding and fried eggs. That breakfast tasted better than anything you got anywhere.

Another report stresses the constant sociality creative of precisely of the sort of communal being-ness we are discussing:

All the people that come down to Market-Town, we meet them in the pubs, and that, and they say that's where they have been to the charity shops, or they have been to the butchers, you know, or they have been to, whatever, the fair, or whatever.

The next quote describes the communal being-ness from the perspective of a young man growing up in the 1960s.

Well we used to have, where the theatre is now, every Saturday night you used to have dances, and the Rolling Stones come here. There was always plenty of dance bands around here and you'd go around the different villages, you know, the dance halls on Friday and Saturday. If you had the money and could get some old pushbike and ride out there.

The following example combines many elements from description of the period: poverty, closeness of space and their centrality within the town.

We used to go and get our broken biscuits to go to the pictures. Then we'd go to [greengrocers] and get a couple of - well it was pennies then - bananas and damaged fruit. That's the only time we could ever really get really nice fruit, the damaged ones. So I used to keep washing and scrubbing all her stairs down 'cause there used to be lino on that then, there was, so I was scrubbing from the top to the bottom and then I'd have my thruppeny piece, go and get my damaged fruit and broken biscuits and then go to the pictures.

Others describe the vibrant life of the town in terms of the centrality of workplaces—factories, railways, central places of industrial work. Reading these reports, one is struck by the sense of Market-Town as a world complete unto itself.

R: *Oh yes. If you wanted to know anything, always go to XXXXs Cafe. He'd have the place out the back, he'd kill the pigs and*

I: *Kill the pigs? They'd kill the pigs there?*

R: *Out the back as well.*

I: *At the back of the cafe? Did they cut their throats or shoot them?*

R: *No, cut their throats.*

I: *What happened to the blood?*

R: *Well that was kept to make black pudding.*

I: *They squealed a lot, did they?*

R: *Yes, I've had to hold them. Well sometimes it takes four of us to hold one, like. They were all around it and the blood would fly, as you can imagine, and it was an honour if the blood hit you. It was great. You used to tell everyone.*

I: *Boys and girls?*

R: *Yeah, just the same, yeah. Because the main thing was to get the head into the bath, not to waste the blood because the blood was valuable.*

Here, we want simply to draw attention to the etched clarity of these images reported to us over 50 years later: the fried egg and the fireman's shovel, the blood stuck in the hair of the laughing children, the broken biscuits. They linger after the telling, so that the particularity of the image becomes almost mythical in its evocation of these worlds and these experiences.

Communal Meaning: The Breathing Space of Working Market-Town

One thing these quotes touch upon is the self-sustaining nature of these towns, something principally provided by the presence of local employment, the closeness of the countryside, and the independence this granted local people.

Work was obviously one central element within the web of relations sustaining of these meanings-in-common, but it needs to be stressed that it wasn't the only thing, nor is it the determining element in any simple sense.

Many statements in the interviews point to ample sources of food, for instance, the river, the summer farm work, the co-operative sharing, the local plots where food was grown. The Henry Street practices of food gathering described in many of our interviews could be argued to have a historical lineage traceable to the pre-enclosure period in Britain. It provided sources of good cheap local food, sources currently unavailable to the estate, most of who rely on stodgy, filling, carbohydrate-based products from the cheapest supermarket.

We mention this now because we are seeking in our account to avoid the sheen of progressivism which sometimes underlines current notions of poverty and the post-war process of slum clearance (Rogaly and Taylor, p. 93).

There often seems to be in these accounts an unspoken assumption which equates processed supermarket food, with progress. As such, it may well be that previous practices provided a better standard of food for the poor than they enjoy currently.

Certainly, work circulated money within the town and certainly, it sustained the materiality evident in the web of relations, but the meanings-in-common were an outcome of the entire range of sociality, the entire linkages and the entire gamut of spaces of appearances. Having work and income simply allowed the communal being-ness that the common sociality created, to expand and be sustained.

Thus the presence of these businesses, particularly the pubs, as well as the local streets around Henry Street with their varied series of accompanying activities, allowed for the multiple construction of being-ness in common through multiple spaces of appearance. This process reinforced the communal being-ness and the sense of commonality and it is through the commonality of experience enacted within the web of relations that communal being-ness is sustained

I realise it now because… how can I say it? There was plenty of work about but the money was very low… First of all I worked for a small firm by the name of xxxs. They used to be in Y Street… you worked six months on a trial before you signed but in the meantime he died and the people that took it over didn't know which way they were going to go; whether to finish the work they had at the factory, so my father had me transferred to [firm] on the … Road. That's where my father worked.

But that's not there anymore, is it.

No, they've finished now. And then there used to be [several firms] but they are all out of business now. It's all one-man concerns now.

It's only the X firm survived.

Yes, …. but Y used to be in obviously. He used to employ a couple of hundred people and customers. You had no trouble in finding work then.

Because even though there wasn't any pits in Market-Town lots of local people, quite a lot in fact, worked up there as well, because it was the main employer until the hospital came along.

Much of this independence and self-sufficiency was of course provided by industries now long disappeared: mines, railways and factories.

Well it was very busy because you had three stations here. You had Breen Road, you had the Millford Road and the Junction. And on a Tuesday and Saturday the people used to come from the farms and the mines down to Market-Town.

Market-Town was replete with local businesses: printing works, small businesses and building firms, as well as the hospital and of course the agriculture going on adjacent to the town. Many interviews described seasonal work in the fields when they could take home produce for themselves.

Apparently, local people were even employed at the Towers Hotel in those days.

And I understand you worked in the Towers Hotel. How did you get a job in there?

Well my mother worked there for years and of course when I was in school I used to go and help clean the potatoes and things. Anyhow, as time went on - and I believe I was about eighteen or twenty - and I went to work in there. But then I was promoted.

So what did you do when you started work there?

I was just a cleaner and potatoes… well doing anything. But I was so good, you see, that they said 'Well we want a chamber maid'.

Did you want the job?

Yes, so I had it.

This was also a much more inclusive world. One in which the working poor exerted their presence through space and the occupation of town's physical geography. The descriptions offered by the first respondent quoted above, a woman who grew up in Henry Street, are characterised by a duality in relation to space. On the one hand there existed wide open spaces: the river meadows and the town, and on the other, the extremely closed spaces of bedrooms and houses, where people lived four or more to a room.

What is clear is that life was lived in public, through endless actions of sociality, actioned in public and held in common.

Kids stealing sweets, kids having to wash the floor, routines performed by women at dinner-time; women standing in the street talking, poaching, self-policing, killing pigs—these are accounts full of intense sociality and the grit of that sociality in a small space and an approximate geography. The impression we get is of a town full of life and activity, full of the action of sociality.

The proximity of people to each other is what links these accounts together. People lived close in the houses of Henry St. The rich and the poor passed close by each other in the town. Many interviews described their fathers as working as gardeners or chauffeurs for the upper classes scattered throughout the countryside around Market-Town.

Henry Street and the river sat side by side. People poached from it and cleaned up after its floods; the railway, and the cottages in the railway terraces, sat close to the factories which circled the town. The presence of one effected and shaped the other; different spaces of appearance jostled and competed in the public plurality afforded by this restricted space and proximate geography.

The next section establishes that these meanings-in-common are active in spaces of appearances in the contemporary present of Market-Town and it does this by comparing the accounts we have just heard with ones collected from an online Facebook site, Forgotten Market-Town.

Facebook

In this section of the chapter, we demonstrate that the town as remembered in interviews also forms a central component of contemporary online discussions of the town. We present examples of these and then go on to think about what this might mean for the present.

The first comment is from the moderator who comments upon the number of times a photo of Henry Street has been viewed.

* *Forgotten Market-Town: Thank you all so much for all the likes and shares - 4,500 people have viewed this picture in the last 24 hours. Wow! Lets hope we can find some more oldies of Henry Street!*
* *My mum's neighbour was the daughter of Mr and Mrs Jones and they lived in Henry Street. He worked in the grocers in town. Best ham on the bone I ever tasted.*
* *I remember Henry Street, could be 50's.*
* *Sure my dad said he was born there.*
* *My grandparents used to keep the [pub] in Henry Street.*
* *Blimey!!! I don't remember it looking like that! Mind you I was never allowed to go down there!!! Hahahaha!!!*
* *I am sure Henry Street was my Gran's home and we lived there when I was born. Can't remember anything, except being pecked by a chicken. Oh, and I think we had the first television in the street and all the neighbours came round to watch some big event (royal, I think).*
* *Who was the pretty girl who worked in the [pub name]*
* *Taken on the eve of the coronation 1 June 1953 by my Father. Henry Street, probably approximately where the police station is to-day.*
* *the shawls*
* *The Xs and Ys lived that end of the street. Big families*
* *I lived in 30 Henry street next door to Mr W. There used to be a shop called …s the second hand shop where we'd get our dresses. Me and my brother would go to the old lodging house to feed the homeless. The [pub name] used to be called the top … The Zs kept it .*
* *Not a memory, but the lady carrying the child in the photo looks exactly like me! Do you know who she is?*
* *My ancestors, c and e, lived in 35 Henry street in the mid 1880's*

- *My mother was a child in Henry street my grandparents lived there the Harris family x sure she got some fab stories about life there x*
- *My grandparents B and E lived there with their children. Will ask my dad if he recognises anyone in the picture*
- *My mother was a child in Henry street my grandparents lived there the H family x sure she got some fab stories about life there x*
- *My mum grew up in Henry street she is one of the k family I used to go see my grandparents there in the 60s and 70s very happy times when my aunties and uncles also visited old nanny k she was a darling and E always in the foresters.*

There are a series of common themes between these quotes communicating across time. The first is clearly family, in the simple sense of recognising relatives and listing them: 'my mum lived there'; 'I'm sure my father was born there', there are many of these. There are other themes around family, big families: the H family, the K family which touches on the statement about the presence and influence of big families historically in Market-Town as well as communication within families across generations: '*Will ask my dad if he recognises anyone in the picture*'

There are other themes: the notion of Henry St as a dangerous space where people were not allowed to go: '*Mind you I was never allowed to go down there!!!*'

A forbidden space which nonetheless has an aura about it and an imaginary quality: '*I don't remember it looking like that*', which could lead one to ask what it did look like in his imagination.

The tales about Henry St seem to already be circulating prior to this post: '*she got some fab stories about life there.*' Shops and places are included with the same sort of sharply etched memories: '*Best ham on the bone I ever tasted*' and being pecked by a chicken. Identifications stretch across time from the 1880s to the 1960s and 1970s. There is even someone who wants to know the name of a woman pictured because she looks exactly like her.

Above all else, there is a sense of Henry St as a space exclusive and unique to itself; a large space in memory and feeling despite its restricted physical geography; a feeling of Henry St and Market-Town centre as a whole, as a homogenous and harmonised single space.

This extract was offered to show how the meanings, not just associated with Henry Street but permeating the entire town, still remain capable of producing action and interest long after the material space has disappeared. In this sense, it taps into the notion of 'deep mapping' mentioned in Chapter 2. Here, the physical structure of the street remains in the memory and, as such, forms an element within the construction of a new space of appearance, this time an online one.

So that while its presence as materiality, as habit, and as working practices (the trains the trains and the factories, the pigs being killed in the back room of the cafe, may have all disappeared, the meanings-in-common which shape social being-ness still exist and, indeed, still shape vast areas of sociality within the town.

Henry St Decanted

The destruction of the three streets around Henry St began sometime in the early 1950s. As a result of the slum clearance of this area, the population were re-located about a mile from the town centre where an estate was planned and built on a bare hill. On the Henry Street site of what was once a thriving communal space, there now stands a police station and a job centre. Apart from that, and despite its proximity to town, there is barely a house on the street.

I: *You said you moved up here when you were five, what year was that?*
R: *'53.*
I: *So they were already building?*
R: *Yes, part of this estate was built.*
I: *How many houses?*
R: *They built up as far as about here.*
I: *From the main road there?*
R: *Yeah, from the road. 'Cause my auntie moved down here in 1949 or '50. And then they built further on up. We came to … st in '53. Then they built … Crescent after that. Then they started building up to the ridge.*
I: *So a gradual kind of where they just added streets as the years went by.*

R: Yes.

I: *And in general you said your grandmother was quite aggrieved. She was aggrieved because… you said she didn't feel lonely but she felt more isolated.*

R: *But she felt isolated a little bit. I think my mother did as well, although we all lived in the same house, and we actually didn't move for a while because my mother wanted to bring… her mother was there and my cousin, because he'd always lived like my brother – that might sound a bit complicated - and she had to wait for the Council to agree to that, which they did eventually.*

I: *Because of course in those days*

R: *It was totally different.*

I: *Your grandmother and mother didn't have a car.*

R: *Oh no, they never had a car, my mother and father.*

I: *So they were much further away from the shops and the market and that sort of thing.*

R: *Yeah. Eventually they put a bus service on.*

I: *And how many years did it take to do that?*

R: *About four or five.*

I: *And the new houses, what were they like? Can you describe what happened when you walked in the door?*

R: *Well if you come from a house that's 140 years old and you walk into a new house you think 'Oh' because the living room probably wouldn't be half of what our old one was. You felt very restricted because our old houses always had quite big rooms; big ceilings. They were massive. And of course there was… I don't know how many rooms. I could count them up. And the bedrooms were an unbelievable size.*

I: *And they all had high ceilings too.*

R: *The thing was a new house: you got an inside bathroom, you got this, a brand new house; you got electric lights - because part of it was still gas lighting.*

Coupled with this gradual adaptation to the estate, its geography and space, the new estate residents all faced changes in the wider world, particularly changes around the type and availability of work.

Well, …s has now closed, as you know, and the hospital is the only other big employer here at the moment, and people get into the hospital jobs, and they seem to stay, you know what I mean? They don't change jobs, and the jobs are advertised internally first, so they seem to go before they are advertised on general, but other than that, there is only really shops, and we have got a precinct, and we have got one, two, three shops have shut down there already, [card shop] is on its way out now.

One result of all of this persistent process of re-location and re-creation, just as it has been throughout Britain, is that by 1990, there remained little physical trace within the town itself, of what had been a living community, barely 30 years before.

The Consequences of Change

The removal of the population from Henry Street to the estate was also the removal of the population from any proximity to services.

The lack of dental and medical services coupled with the lack of shops, supermarkets or even a pub, means that the estate is constructed as removed from the town and yet entirely dependent upon it.

The capacity to influence the town simply by their centrality and their occupation of space is also denied by apparatus of power within the town, as well as the demarcation invented by the county, which places a third of the estate within an adjoining jurisdiction, creating a situation in which, as one councillor put it, 'the estate is someone else's problem'. A starker contrast to their previous situation in Henry St could hardly be imagined and it is hard to believe that it is entirely the outcome of coincidence and chance.

The young girl we met earlier who cried, walking to school from the estate after her family moved there, who cried every morning because it was so far to walk, became the head of the local high school management committee as well as the head of several housing co-ops, volunteer organisations and intervention projects on the estate.

I: And it was compulsory to move, wasn't it?
N1:   Yes, you had to move. You had no choice. They condemned the houses, wholesale. This is how they broke the community up. They didn't move,

say, a block of houses all together and keep the community together; they just moved them and scattered them.
I: *Why do you think they did that?*
N1:   *I don't know.*
I: *Well, you've had a lot of time to think about it.*
N1:   *I think they wanted to break Henry Street apart.*

Statistics tell the story about the estate in relation to the rest of the county, though of course these figures are extremely hard to locate in their totality, both because the overall county is so wealthy that it conceals the depth of deprivation on the estate and secondly because the estate itself, as it features in the statistics, is administratively split into different areas so that a general picture is difficult to establish. Ratings in terms of the index of multiple deprivation (IMD) show that the area covered by the government anti-poverty initiative mentioned in Chap. 3, an area which includes the estate, is

- 150 times worse in terms of access to services than the rest of the county
- 900 times worse in terms of community safety
- 450 times worse in education
- 700 times worse in employment
- 1000 times worse in health
- 250 times worse in housing
- 450 times worse in income
- 1000 times worse in physical environment
- The highest domestic violence rates in the county

One will never know how these statistics measure against the 'deprivation' of Henry Street. However, there is also no evidence that they are in fact any better than Henry St. Certainly, they are, just in themselves, a telling indicator of the failure of progressivist rhetoric.

Yet at least three people from the town told us in interviews and conversations that in fact there was no poverty on the estate. Indeed, as we shall examine next, the level of almost wilful ignorance in the town concerning conditions on the estate is shocking in itself.

This is a situation which could be argued is a direct outcome of the initial move up the hill.

Certainly, access to services and physical environment, two elements in the IMD, must have been better for Henry Street, regardless of any other elements, simply because Henry Street was located in the centre of the town.

This exclusion and isolation imposed upon the estate can be seen in any number of comments made to us by respondents.

The voluntary member of the local housing association had this to say:

I: *Yea, and you have got the leisure centre down here.*
R: *if you are from here, they don't want you down there you know.*

In all of this, it is hard not to see a certain malice towards Henry Street, particularly given the progressive stripping of Market-Town assets by the county and the county dominated town council over the last 30 years.

The contrast with Henry Street and its position in the centre of town is stark. Something shown clearly in this quote from a middle-aged estate resident when asked about things to do when she was growing up in the terraces around Morgan Street where the railway workers lived:

R: *there were always things to do there., cycling clubs; the Scouts; the Guides; the St John's Ambulance. There was dancing going on and there was always something going on between streets in Market-town. Soap-box derbies is what I used to do a lot of.*

She goes on to speak of the current estate explicitly in regard to the situation for children and teenagers:

I   *Are any of those things like scouts or boys brigade around here now?*
J: *No, they are all down in the middle of town, they're down in the ...., a lot of people can't afford to use them, there is charges now for them to go to, you know, it's all changed.*
I: *And you think it is basically the fact that people charge now?*
J: *A lot of families can't afford it, it's the uniform they have got to buy, and you know, and if they are going on trips, it is a lot of money, and espe-cially now the way things are.*

What seeped out of these interviews was the sour truth that despite the endless efforts of many on the estate to help the estate and to improve their own homes, efforts we saw almost on a daily basis, the combination of abstract economic forces and actions local and far away, constantly undermined and stifled them.

The next section examines how the meanings-in-common derived from Henry Street and indeed that period of the town's history are nowadays excluded from the discourses of Market-Town.

Exclusion of This Meaning-in-Common from Town Life

This section looks at the ways in which the public, 'official' memory of Market-Town has been shorn of the meanings-in-common associated with Henry Street and the working past of the town. It looks at the effect of this removal and the outcomes that have flowed from that for the town itself.

The major effect of removal of the poor working population to the outskirts of town has been an increase in the divisions between the town and those 'up the hill'.

M: *Poor people on the estate, the reservation, the locals call it.*
I: *Do they?*
M: *Yea, I only heard that within the last week or two, it's the reservation [laughter]*

This quote says it all. Moreover, it was a nick-name repeated frequently to us by others who lived in the pre-60's boundaries of the town—the boundaries which once included Henry Street.

In regard to the quote, we ask a simple question: when Henry Street was situated in the middle of town, would it have been referred to in these terms, as 'the reservation'

Somehow, we doubt it.

It is a fair assumption that this has arisen since Henry Street was relocated up the hill and out of town. Let us also consider what a 'reservation' actually is.

From Wikipedia (https://en.wikipedia.org/wiki/Indian_reservation), we learn that Native American reservations

> were created on lands that were deemed worthless to white settlers, meaning they were often uncultivable, resource deficient, and isolated from urban centers and transportation networks.
>
> On large reservations, the extreme poverty rate is as much as six times the national rate.
>
> In addition to poverty rates, reservations are hindered by low education levels, poor healthcare services, low employment, substandard housing, and deficient economic infrastructure.

Sociologist Loic Wacquant (2010) has described reservations as areas of 'socio-spatial seclusion', where residents are corralled and isolated, and claims that the reservations were created to immobilise native peoples.

Given the statistics from the IMD noted earlier, such a comparison is perhaps more apt than many realise.

The Role of the Heritage Industry

In common with market-towns all over Britain, our particular Market-Town has pursued a policy of strengthening tourism and heritage as a means of generating income. Much of this is seen as a substitute for the industries and services that previously employed the bulk of the population.

As was noted previously, one aspect of this is the annual festival. Other aspects include steam train festivals, Shire horse shows and, recently, national bike trials and various national competitions. Much fuss is made of these and during the period of our investigation, breathless reports would reach us via various councillors regarding the locating of some facility of a sporting or cultural sort in the surrounding county and the great benefits which would flow to the town as a result.

Characteristically, however, these events, rather than bringing the town together, tended to emphasise the divisions within it. Some aspects of this were discussed in the last chapter in relation to the festival. A recent much-heralded bike race also illustrates this succinctly. For the weekend of the races, local streets were closed, sometimes for 10–12 hours during the day and care workers and council services were unable to access homes in the course of their duties. Residents complained of insufficient consultation and in five places around the county, tacks were laid on the road as a form of protest. Indeed, in one county village, a number of arrests were made when locals protesting the holding of the race and causing inconvenience reportedly pelted the riders with fruits and rocks.

A number of commentators (Smith, Shackel, and Campbell; Waterton Emma and Watson Steve 2011; Wedgewood, T. 2009) have discussed the manner in which local hierarchies can impede the ability of working-class groups to be given recognition in heritage and cultural narratives. By using our analytic, we can see what is excluded from this heritage perspective, how indeed local hierarchies impose their own meanings-in-common upon those present within the town by excluding meanings-in-common stemming from Henry Street and a working past.

We saw how the 'Forgotten Market-Town' Facebook site gained and sustained great success in the town by concentrating upon personal narratives, oral history, and by touching into the meanings-in-common and the communal memory neglected by the heritage and cultural perspective of the moneyed web of relations. How by showing pictures of the open-air pool and Henry Street, it developed linkages into a meaning-in-common absent from the official narrative.

Emma Waterton (2010) has recently noted that the paradox within the heritage industry's perceived inclusiveness of 'public heritage' is that currently there is no distinct role for 'the public' within the management process. This is certainly confirmed by the experience within Market-Town, where meanings-in-common particular to much of Market-Town's past are utterly absent from any of the 'official' heritage or cultural narratives.

Instead, the council focuses, at least in its heritage displays, on what Kynan Gentry (2013) terms a nineteenth-century view, where the social elites concentrate primarily upon historic sites and buildings, which they view as powerful symbols of the intellectual and social hegemony of the educated middle class and their cultural values. This certainly remains the case in Market-Town as the letter from the local historian and the tourist literature makes abundantly clear.

Not only does this rather antiquated approach (ibid) not strengthen community ties and community organisation or enhance the identity and unique character of communities but it also flies in the face of available evidence concerning what local communities want. A Heritage Commission study of the Australian town of Queanbeyan (Walker 1988), for instance, found that the community tended to value places not so much for their architecture or historical value, but as part of their communal being-ness in the ongoing life of the town, and as reminders of significant events in their own lives. This is something which our research indicates is precisely the situation in Market-Town.

Indeed, it could be argued that current town strategies of heritage, culture and tourism simply alienate the majority of the town's population, return very little to them by way of additional income, and increases the town population's distance from council and government generally.

This description is precisely the case, for instance, with the festival: an event too expensive for many locals to attend and from which, at least according to local shopkeepers, little of the profits are retained in the town.

Once again, the narrow perspective of the town council and its continued domination by the county has meant that the town itself, its well-being, its financial and social needs, its history are excluded from the perspective of town officials with a resultant undermining of local faith in the council itself.

'The Town's Not What It Was, That's for Sure'

Having discussed the meanings-in-common associated with Henry Street and then the effect of these in the town, we want to sum up this section by including comments about the town in the contemporary world. Some interview comments give the flavour of one aspect of this. These are all responses from different people.

> *Town's going downhill rapid. They don't make decisions at the local level see. That council don't consider health of the community., They only care about the money. The shops are closing, all these holes in the pavement.*

Shopping's getting worse I know that. Really it's got worse over the last thirty years. They knocked down the newspaper office and built Tescos. They have to listen…. listen more but they don't.

The main street's gone to ruin I tell a you that.

There's a lack of trust see because it don't matter who you vote for. They've wrecked the town, split the feeling the ethos of it!

They're taking away the market you know the open air market —what's a market town without a market. They're killing it bit by bit.

Well, they run the market down, I mean they wanted to get rid of the market nearly ten years ago, but they couldn't close the market, so what do they do? Run it down, so they reckon now it's beyond repair like, too expensive.

There's black clouds over Market-Town with the selling of the Stock Market. Market-Town is an historic place. Take the market out and the heart of the town will be gone.

One of the constant themes resonating through all the interviews was the decline of the town as a public space.

Very few local people had a good word to say about the current shopping precinct. These comments were regularly accompanied by specific, commonly utilised examples: too many charity shops; closure of the livestock market; presence of supermarkets; decisions of the council.

Most responses dated this decline to the post-1980s, and most accompanied their criticisms with reference to the wonderful spirit and friendliness of the people of Market-Town.

Additionally, there is a clear lack of trust between the population and the town council. It is clearly expressed in the 'them' and 'us' mentality which runs through these quotes.

Of course, it is easy to dismiss all of this as nostalgia. Certainly, those are the terms which the council use when confronted with these sorts of criticisms (as do academic commentators: Rose 1999; Bauman 2001).

Yet to us, this criticism appears superficial. Superficial, firstly, because these responses characteristically list contemporary buildings or spaces which have either disappeared or appeared in that space as replacement. It is thus a view grounded in the world of Market-Town as it is *now*, and the past is used to critique the present. The past and the present exist inter-relationally. This becomes clearer when the talk turns to the future of the livestock market, a recent contentious topic in the town.

Secondly, the descriptions of the material commonality of the town and the state of its current situation are also combined with effusive praise for the current people of the town, praise crucially framed in terms of sociality, spirit, friendliness and nature.

Although a lot of Market-Town was altered, there are still some nice things here. It's a town I'd recommend anybody to visit, from anywhere. There's some lovely walks. They've got some lovely things going on, even pantomimes in the town hall. The majority of Market-Town people, when you approach them, are civilised people. They're nice people to talk to.

So, the fact that these interviews are taking place now in an inter-relational public space, a space of appearance, and given these speech-acts are in response to specific questions concerning that inter-relationality and space as it exists around them in the present, it is clear that they are much more than simply a passive longing for the past—they are an action in the present. These responses of action–speech are created from the action of sociality in the present. As such, this action is containing of all elements of personal being-ness entwined with the communal being-ness history of the sociality and the town in which it occurs.

These responses are the living plurality of the town expressing its communal being-ness in common and, in turn, re-creating and thus maintaining its own being-ness in common through the action of speech.

That is why it makes much more sense, we would argue, to see these responses as critiques - critiques which draw upon precisely the meanings-in-common, memories and communal feelings we have been exploring. These meanings-in-common thus explain space and communal reality *in the present*, much in the manner that people draw on personal experience to explain current predicaments or mathematicians draw on previous proofs to advance their understanding of complex theorems.

Finally, these criticisms as a critique are supported by the responses of young people who also find the town dead and empty and who do so without any historical yardstick, but who, rather, see it as it is within their short lifetime.

'Best place to hang out?'—'Nowhere'
'Where is the best place to go?' 'Nowhere to go'

Over and over again, the simple, repeated litany concerns the lack of facilities, the lack of shopping and the council's lack of care for the town.

There's nowhere for us to go except the park and when it rains we can't even go into the park.

As one respondent noted—'*Market-Town excludes its young people*'. Many of all ages reported that they shopped out of town in nearby supermarkets, often in towns smaller than Market-Town. The town council is constantly pre-occupied with 'shopping', parking, the main street, tourism and the general consumer, and have been so pre-occupied for a very long time, many decades in fact. Yet all their efforts have been, from the perspective of the town itself, a spectacular failure, an irony which has not stopped or even checked the focus of the town council who appear blithely unaware of this failure to convince.

Our entire argument is amply illustrated by one simple fact: in the 1960s, the town hall was used for popular local dances, yet when we ran the play described below, almost all the people who attended from the estate reported to us that they had never set foot inside the town theatre. This is a stark illustration of the degree to which these meanings-in-common associated with Henry Street and working Market-Town have regressed from the town's public space of appearance.

Continuing Presence of These Communal Meanings

As we have argued, it would be easy to dismiss these discussions of the working of the town centre as nostalgia. However, we want to present it in a different way. We have argued that just because a form of community is not obvious now, it does not mean that the communal being-ness is dead.

Rather, we argue that communal being-ness is constantly present and therefore one has to understand the forms that this being-ness takes at any one moment. However, this should not blind us to the fact that the shift in communal being-ness over historical time is produced by political policy, not as some naturalised effect of a benign history or the removed effect of some hidden abstract law like economic forces. Nor should it be de-politicised with a normative psychologism like 'nostalgia'. Political decisions are choices made by social power and the expulsion of communal meanings from the lived space of the town is the direct result of choices made by the town and county council.

We might ask what it meant to assume that progress is served by breaking up communal being-ness, especially when the communal being-ness around Henry St presented as an advanced form of social solidarity, social co-operation and social power.

We might ask what it means to forcibly re-locate this to the periphery. When we consider the move to finance capital, we might also think of the moment of the conservative introduction of neo-liberalism and the significance of the rise of a working population that, at that exact moment, were actually managing to make some kind of living and some improvements in their own lives.

What we need to bear in mind is that the effects of these historical shifts is to empty the centre of Market-Town that there are basically no spaces for the working people of Market-Town to meet easily outside the home. Not one pub or social club exists on the estate. Many of the pubs in the town centre have been closed, theatres where dances were held are now non-existent as spaces for this types of activity, so that after the end of the working day there is literally no public social space left in which to meet. This forces the population to the periphery and into their own homes and streets.

Of course, the forced re-location to the estate is not solely to blame for this, rather that move combined with all the other developments we have described together contributed to what was a slow decline.

At first the re-located estate simply continued to come into town to work and to meet, but gradually over that 30-year period, the sites for sociality have been severely reduced—either as an outcome of different forms of policing or the influx of commercialisation which sealed away sites previously shared, or simply by the re-development of the town as a site for outside visitors under the guise of tourism.

The combined effect of this however is that the town centre is now, particularly at night, simply a hollow vacuum and the town has no place for the estate and the Henry Street meanings, while the working people have no place in it either, except as day-time consumers.

The spaces that still exist—for example, the Towers Hotel and the Theatre have operated as zones of exclusion for the mass of the population. The theatre that was once a popular dance-hall now offers fare that is too expensive and socially exclusionary.

'Up the Estate'

The building which houses the theatre also serves as the venue for town council meetings. A Victorian brownstone building in the centre of the town, it reflects all the civic pride, exclusion and prosperity of its Victorian origins.

The theatre itself marks clearly a shift towards a tourist orientation: a polite, institutional and heritage status. Events are seated, middlebrow plays by Noel Coward, television comedians on book tours; tribute bands, trad jazz nights and children's shows fill the programme of coming attractions. The need to fill seats, the heritage, monument, and tourist element couple very nicely with contemporary economic and social thinking. It has also had the effect of entirely removing the estate and the Market-Town working population from any attendance or use of the theatre.

The play we staged, entitled 'Up the Estate', came about based on an idea suggested by the estate steering committee. Together the steering committee hired a theatre director who gave the uttered and recorded stories of people from the estate a dramatic structure, wrote songs, rehearsed actors from the estate, and brought in good amateur and a few professional actors for a single performance at the Market-Town theatre.

The free-ticketed play was sold out, 70 % of the audience being from the estate. Many self-reported that they had never been into the Market-Town theatre before.

It is clear from the reports of the researchers who sat in the audience during the performance, that there was among the audience, as one person put it, 'a fair bit of sniffling going on'.

The play traced the history of the estate from its creation in the early 1950s to the present day. It dealt with the ambiguous and mixed feelings many had about leaving Henry Street and the centre of town. It showed the path of one family who were re-located, from their early delight at possessing indoor plumbing through their unemployment, their children, their son's tours of Northern Ireland, and events like marriages and Christmases. The audience from the estate saw their own lives, saw their own children acting out their own lives. Adults from the estate ran the event backstage while young people from the estate acted their roles with intensity and success.

The theatre during that evening performance was a space of appearance productive of a being-ness held in common, created from the sociality of the play and the audience, in a space where action and containment created a communal meaning, held co-operatively by the 'audience'. And this communal meaning was the development of meanings of Henry Street and the working people of Market-Town.

What it illustrated clearly was that these meanings-in-common - the meanings-in-common of the Henry Street communal being-ness-had not disappeared, but rather they have 'been disappeared'. That their absence from the centre of the town was not their choice but something imposed upon them. That as such, 'community' has not gone, as lots of commentators superficially assert, but rather it has been removed, as an act of wilful social power.

Online Spaces for the Enactment of Meanings-in-Common

Forgotten Market-Town Facebook Site

Another space of appearance that supports our main contention is the online Facebook 'Forgotten Market Town' mentioned earlier. In this section, we will consider this site as a space of appearance in which the communal meanings derived and created through the history of the working people of Market-Town can be aired. When the argument is made about online communities, it is not often considered that maintaining a form of sociality that once was in the streets may now only be possible in the home and thus maintaining contact online in a form that re-enacts a sociality as it was is the only way in which those excluded can claim the ghost of a space they once inhabited.

If this is nostalgia (which we dispute), then it longs for and attempts to continue to create a communal being-ness in the now—a being-ness in common even amidst its own confinement.

Let us look firstly at the figures for this social media site which are impressive in themselves. As of August 2014, the Forgotten Market-Town site had

- 3021 'Likes' and an average of 3100 views per post.
- Between September 2013 when it was inaugurated and June 2014, it has been viewed 300,000 times and it averages 7500 views per week.
- Each post has drawn an average of 18 comments per post and again on average, it has 1200 active viewers per week.
- Originating from the site but measured across all platforms for inter-inked social media, it has achieved a combined total of 400,000 plus views across all Forgotten Market-Town channels: Facebook, Twitter, Google+, You Tube and Blogger.
- Its highest viewed post accumulated 16,350 views and across all pages on all media it has an average of 7500 views.
- 59 % of its followers are women and 41 % men. Its highest user group are women aged 25–34 who constitute 15 % of users. Its lowest user group are men aged 65 plus who constitute 2 % of users.
- It accumulates, on the average, 25 new 'Likes' a week.

Forgotten Market-Town has also integrated itself firmly into the community.

- There are 15 local community groups actively engaged and submitting content
- Schoolchildren from five local schools using Forgotten Market-Town as part of their curriculum

- 18 local businesses use Forgotten Market-Town content to strengthen their organisation
- Partnership working with approximately 25 Market-Town based businesses and media sources

These figures are extremely impressive for a community Facebook site dedicated to a specific community. Indeed the 3000 plus 'likes' represent over a quarter of the Market-Town population.

By using 'call to action' messages, encouraging followers to share posts and to 'Like' posts, Forgotten Market-Town has grown, organically and communally, without paid advertising or indeed any aspect of the narrow online business model. It thus stands in contradistinction from the model of sociality underlying council decisions over the last 30 years.

Sharing of posts is a good indicator of this aspect of interest. Facebook insights show that between September 2013 and June 2014, post shares varied between 5 and 330. The more popular topics for 'shares' included historic pictures of local buildings, pubs, allotments, swimming pools, markets, and so on, many of which have disappeared.

The success of this project reveals a strong desire for local people to link with and understand their own environs and their part and place in it - all of which was evident in the earlier posts regarding Henry Street. It shows that the communal being-ness centred around Henry street and the meanings-in-common associated with that finds a ready audience within the town, primarily because it taps into a communal being-ness and forms of sociality and communal meanings by offering an open space where that sociality is recognised and can flourish. Thus, the site serves to link an existing but largely conversational commonality with its historical antecedents, while enhancing, materialising and expanding that communal being-ness through the repetitive sociality of the site itself, something illustrated clearly in the earlier Henry Street extract.

On the site itself, the style of post and the style of comment are central to understanding this success. Both are vastly different from the sort of history expressed in local museums. The conversations are personal, written in a colloquial language; they stress participation through families, through stories, and through direct experience. In doing so, they assert a casual but authentic ownership of the events being described. In general, the more public the building displayed in a photo, the more comments and shares the post draws.

In this regard, it is clear that Forgotten Market-Town draws upon a pre-existing web of communal feeling, something also evident in the inherent understanding often displayed concerning what comments 'mean'. Spelling mistakes are rife and there is little punctuation—all of which confirms the friendly, comfortable sense emanating from these comments as well as the shared perspective of communal meanings in common.

These comments represent the memories of family, friends, rituals of childhood and cultural practice; certain people are named and located in time and space. The comments establish linkages across generations and between decades, the interweaving of comments up and down the page establish a social meaning held in common, or rather it shapes and constructs another element of that being-ness in common, one particular to the existing web of town communal meanings.

Of course, these meanings-in-common are not the sort likely to feature heavily at the Towers Hotel, nonetheless they are held in common among many within the town, as the success of the Facebook site illustrates.

The forum this site provides for all ages to inter-act is increasingly rare in this individualised and demarcated society. Indeed, one of the characteristics of 'Forgotten Market-Town' illustrated in these comments is precisely the manner in which all age groups appear equally fascinated by their own history and the social process which allows these groups to appear in public side by side. The presence of one memory allows others to reconstruct a longer broader version of their own communal history—a communal view of the town as more democratic, more inclusive, more personal, more open to a plurality of being-ness held in common. Indeed all over the country, similar Facebook pages are springing up in which ordinary people share their memories of place, all driven by the same motivation.

This is reflected in the sorts of people who participate and post or comment on the site. They are clearly working people or from that background. There is little competition between comments, no one is challenged about their right to participate or recall, as was the case with the letter from the local historian. In the two years of this site's operation, there has never been a moderated comment, a troll or an outburst of anger directed at another poster. All the comments are posted under people's real names and this in itself makes the site unique. It also confirms the communal nature of the posts. People want to be linked to others under their own name. It also confirms Arendt's point about meaning-in-common as an outcome of being-ness before others *in public*.

The huge response to this site from within the town confirms the principal point, which is that the communal being-ness of the working people of Market-Town once contained within a manifested and physical web of relations, continues to exist and influence sociality in the contemporary world long after the materiality of that communal being-ness and web of relations has disappeared.

That communal being-ness is not an historical relic consigned to the dust-bin but rather maintains its capacity to mobilise around and generate new communal meanings, meanings-in-common and the sociality required to established more being-ness in common. All of this is evident once it is provided a public space to do so.

So the Forgotten Market-Town page illustrates the continued survival and presence of Henry Street and its meanings-in-common in a stark and powerful form.

Conclusion

Market-Town is a very different town from daytime to evening. During the day, the streets tend to feature working-class people, families, either from the estate or from the surrounding areas, as well as the young and the lower-income retirees. There is a lot of sociality and conversation; there are office workers, shop workers, buskers and people greeting and chatting away.

In the evenings, the pedestrianised area is much more sparsely populated, the older pubs are almost empty, no shops are open, and apart from around the theatre, there is little evidence of any activity. At this time, the only people who are commonly seen are the utter opposite of the daytime crowd: they tend to be middle-aged, well dressed in suits or expensive-looking outfits with well-presented hair. They tend to be in couples, and aside from them, the town for all intents and purposes is a dead space.

As the preceding chapters make clear, this situation is a recent thing. Indeed, according to H1 as recently as the 1990s when she was in her late teens, the complete opposite was the case. All the pubs in town were heaving with people, the restaurants too—people spilled into the streets from the wine bars and restaurants.

There are a number of reasons for this emptying of public life from Market-Town, no single cause explains everything. The advent of Wetherspoons with its cheap beer prices stripped customers from many of the older pubs but even Wetherspoons nowadays is often sparsely inhabited. The economic downtown has certainly contributed, but once again, according to accounts, this decline has been ongoing since around 2000, that is, before the financial crisis of 2008.

In any case, whatever the particular causes, what our work suggests is something far deeper. For what our research indicates is that over the last 30 years, the public spaces of the town have been progressively closed to the communal being-ness of the majority of Market-Town inhabitants.

Whatever the specific rationale behind these decisions and whatever their apparent differences, the results are identical: a certain mode of sociality, a mode which we have labelled for ease of reference as 'Henry Street', the mode of communal being-ness *specific* to Market-Town, and its historical being-ness, is denied spaces in the town for its communal expression and thus denied spaces for the maintenance and creation of its own communal specificity and being-ness. The result is a vacuum, a lifeless space, where the capacity of communal meanings to exert its presence through sociality within the town is denied and the capacity for communal self-help arising from the creation of communal meaning is vastly diminished.

Perhaps this is why some sociologists claim that community no longer exists or that it has disappeared. We would say not that community has disappeared, but rather that it has *been disappeared.* Our research shows clearly the continuing presence of community within the town, just as it also shows that the sociality necessary for the ongoing creation of that communal being-ness constructive of 'community' has been denied spaces for its own expression. This means that, in many ways, Market-Town has become a site closed to the expression of its own communal being-ness.

Bibliography

Gentry, K. (2013). History, heritage and localism. *Policy Studies, 34*(5–6), 508–522.

Rose, N. (1999). *Powers of freedom*. Cambridge: Cambridge University Press.

Smith, L., Shackle, P. A., & Campbell, G. (2011). *Heritage, labour and the working class*. London: Routledge.

Wacquant, L. (2010). Designing urban seclusion in the twenty-first century. *The Yale Architectural Journal, 164*–175.

Walker. (1988). *A heritage commission study of the Australian town of Queanbeyan.*

Waterton, E., & Smith, L. (2010). The recognition and misrecognition of community heritage. *International Journal of Heritage Studies, 16*(1–2), 4–15.

Waterton, E., & Watson, S. (2011). *Heritage and community engagement: Collaboration or contestation*. London: Routledge.

Wedgwood, T. (2009). History in Two Dimensions or Three? Working Class Responses to History. *International Journal of Heritage Studies, 15*(4), 277–297.

Part III

Communal Being-ness and Social Policy

7

Volunteering: Governmentality and Communal Meanings

The previous two chapters examined the actioning of informal communal meanings through the continual production of being-ness in various spaces of appearance. Chapters 5 and 6 explored the way in which communal meanings manifest as social power or indeed, in the case of Henry Street, as social dispowerment.

Both chapters illustrate how the 'community' of Market-Town, its common being-ness, is not the simple outcome of any single strand of commonality, be it location or interest, but rather gains its common being-ness inter-relationally from all elements existent within their recurring number of spaces of appearance.

Commonality is created in the specificity of sociality and cannot be reduced to a simple descriptor of location or interest. The starting point is relationality, so relationality is the driving force, not **a** person, **a** place or **a** thing.

As the product of inter-relationality, being-ness is a constantly moving aspect sustained and sustaining of the commonality of the web of relations. Thus, communal being-ness is also a specific moment in that

© The Author(s) 2016
D. Studdert, V. Walkerdine, *Rethinking Community Research*,
DOI 10.1057/978-1-137-51453-0_7

creation, subject to ongoing re-configurations in exactly the same manner as being-ness in common.

As such communal being-ness like being-ness in common is always fluid and should be understood as part of a constantly changing web.

In light of these conclusions, what this chapter examines are the 'formal', rather than the 'informal', means for constructing communal and particular being-ness.

Our analytic will build once again from the same simple formula:

Sociality = action + containment = being-ness in common/meanings-in-common + repetition = communal being-ness.

The initial part of this chapter will do two things. Firstly, it will use data to examine volunteering from the level of sociality and the space of appearance, and examine this data to provide an image of volunteering as an action within a space of appearance.

Secondly, while doing this first task, it will note and discuss, among other things, the function of containment, the place of the state in our contemporary commonality, the existence and activity of communal meanings, as well as the inter-relationality of the communal meanings of governmentality with the estate's communal being-ness, and draw conclusions regarding the general communal being-ness of the Market-Town estate.

The State as Containment

Earlier we noted that unfinalisable action always required containment. In contemporary society, the primary means for the species containment of unfinalisable action is governmentality and its legal and policy framework.

What we will demonstrate in this chapter is how the state acts within a space of appearance in the same manner and towards the same end as the mode of practice termed by Arendt, the household, the same 'household' we observed in the Tescos example.

In short, we will explore how the household attempts to close the space of appearance through the continual production of a specific being-ness in common.

As we saw in Chap. 3, one common characteristic of the household was its claim of universal authority and the primacy it afforded abstraction over action. Household authority is universalised across spaces of appearance and is sovereign in every situation. It is productive of being-ness in common and meaning-in-common.

Of course, the contemporary European state, with its highly developed web of relations, its history, its honed demarcations, and its vocabulary of abstraction (e.g. 'society', 'accountability' and 'national interest'), always presents itself as the exclusive, representative and sovereign voice of the social world, the ultimate voice in the containment of action and the ultimate authority dictating the terms for the construction of being-ness in common and hence of communal being-ness.

Yet, as we have seen, there are infinite sites for the construction of communal being-ness, infinite combinations of containment and action and manifold sites for the construction of being-ness in common.

There is never a single defining voice, capable of entirely dictating the terms of appearance for being-ness in common. The household, as we saw with the Tescos 'script', can never control absolutely every space of appearance. There are multiple elements in every construction of being-ness in common, just as there are multiple actions of sociality.

Being-ness held in common is the temporary outcome of inter-relationality between many competing strands of meanings-in-common, of which only one, we would argue, is the particular form of communal being-ness proposed by governmentality.

The forms of containment endorsed by governmentality for the shaping of action are simply strands (albeit of the more powerful variety) among many other inter-relational strands. What Foucault calls governmentality can therefore also be understood as a form of meaning-in-common.

Using the analytic outlined earlier, this chapter investigates opposing governmental and informal communal meanings evoked in the action of being-ness creation, to establish evidentially the claims asserted in the previous three paragraphs.

It shows how contrasting communal meanings strive to exert themselves within the construction of being-ness in common. An understanding which, hopefully, also casts light on the place of governmentality within our overall communal being-ness.

In investigating the inter-relationality between the formal communal meanings of governmentality and the informal communal meanings, the chapter therefore simultaneously engages with the actions, limits and capacities of governmentality, as a household power, and its capacity to achieve its desired outcomes within particular actions of sociality.

It shows how attempts by the formal meanings of governmentality to construct being-ness-in-common within the space of appearance are themselves counterpointed and contained by action as well as other communal meanings also present within the same space. Thus, it shows that the construction of being-ness is a far more complex interaction than the mode defined either by the state/individual axis or by notions of governmentality and subject.

Volunteering: Context

In the last 20 years, volunteering has often been presented as one response to a wide range of social and political problems, including unemployment and social disenchantment (Milligan and Fyfe 2004).

In particular, since the highly influential work of David Putnam (1993, 2000), volunteering has been overwhelmingly theorised in terms of participation in a pre-defined public life (Portes A (2000); Evers 2003; Devine and Roberts 2003).

A brief description of one scheme will show how this translates into governmental policy and practice.

Following the general election of 2010, the Conservative/Liberal coalition government unveiled its 'Big Society' plan. The plan proposed 'a new era of people power' where volunteers take over services previously provided by the government. Unrolled in an era of 'Austerity', the plan proposed training local citizens, especially young people, giving financial support to mutuals, co-operatives, charities and social enterprises to take over and run public services, and giving a general power of competence to local councils (https://www.gov.uk/government/publications/building-the-big-society 2010). It was driven by the idea that 'rolling back big government' will lead 'communities' to start running public services themselves (Ibid).[1]

To this end, the Big Society programme promised action in three areas:

- Community empowerment described by the Government as 'local people taking control of how things are done in their area and being helped to do so by local government and others'
- Opening up public services described by the Government as 'public sector organisations and individuals demonstrating innovative ways of delivering public services and charities, social enterprises and private companies showing new ways of delivering public services'
- Social action defined by the Government as 'people being, and being encouraged to be, more involved in their communities through giving time, money and other resources'

Many commentators (Rose 1999; Young 1999) have questioned the abstractions and the slogans in which announcements of the Big Society sort are routinely couched. Many have suggested that this shows a hidden agenda.

What we want to examine here, however, are the terms for the construction of being-ness in common in one space of appearance connected to the 'Big Society'.

To do this, we want to begin with the notion of volunteering as it is contained and presented in the Big Society programme. We will argue that this programme and 20 years of similar programmes preceding it conceal a subtle but significant shift in the use of the term volunteer (Hendrill, Baines and Wilson 2008).

Previously, volunteering was much closer in practice to mutual aid—given freely of time to help a wide variety of organisations embedded in a local community. As we shall see, there remain many, many situations of

---

[1] In truth, for all this fanfare, what the Big Society represented was a continuation of programmes and approaches developed under previous governments, including Tony Blair's Third Way, New Labour's 'parents reading pledge', and various other initiatives.

this sort in Market-Town: boy scouts, pensioners' dinners, park upkeep, kayak clubbing, bike riding clubs, the history society, to name a few. All of which are sustained by this sort of volunteer mutual aid and support. As we will also show, many of these organisations operate with a good deal, more efficiency and more impact than the semi-private, semi-public organisations, public services, charities, social enterprises and private companies favoured by the 'Big Society'.

In comparison, government programmes like the 'Big Society', have sort to formalise the notion of volunteering. Within this policy literature, volunteering becomes an action, pre-emptively and universally defined. Indeed, even 'social action' is defined and, in the process, narrowed to 'giving time, money and other resources'. These are both separate actions conjointly constructive of a potential space of appearance. Discursively, governmentality identifies a virtual figure and builds its validated sociality around the being-ness of this volunteer.

Of equal importance, the being-ness-in-common of a volunteer can now only be enunciated in specific, designated spaces of appearance: organisational structures, typically directly funded projects; community initiatives funded, but not directly run, by government; private charities, co-operatives, mutual associations and social enterprises as nominated by appropriate level of government.[2]

In practice, despite the alphabet of names, these organisations share many similarities: routinely they are either funded directly or indirectly by some government agency; they usually employ several professionals, and, crucially, they typically rely on unpaid volunteers for a so-called service delivery.

In practice, the construction of the rules for the space and the space itself go hand in hand. Governance appears on the estate in a material and subjective mode.

Thus, the state has produced a space of appearance productive of a being-ness in common, termed 'volunteerism'.

---

[2] Given the plethora of organisations constituting the voluntary sector, our account, for the sake of convenience, will be following Baines, Hardrill and Wilson (2011), who refer to all these 'community interventions' as one entity: Voluntary and Community Sector (abbreviated to [VCS]).

Volunteering exists now as an outcome of specific actions enacted within that specific space of appearance. It provides time and works towards a specific pre-defined aim.

To strengthen the creation of being-ness, included in this nominated space, there are of course the detritus of governance: the pseudo-legality of health and safety, mission statements, performance indicators, workplace safety, budgetary transparency and funding applications. All support the space as a household, productive of being-ness in common.

This re-casting of volunteering as a governmental meaning-in-common is of course a re-casting proposed against something else.

This something else is, as we saw earlier, the more traditional idea of volunteering, forms more like gift giving, associated with mutual support and identification with the needs of others in one's locality.

Baines and Hardrill (ibid) locate this mode of volunteering primarily within 'disadvantaged communities', apparently, given their lack of definition, a self-evident term. However, we would contest the notion that these older traditions are simply the particular province of disadvantaged communities whatever they may be.[3] Historically, there are many traditions of volunteering across all classes, and all the traditions speak equally of elements associated with mutual aid and self-help, including among the rich (http://www.success.com/article/16-rich-habits).

What we do want to stress, however, is that there exist distinct and varied traditions of volunteering and that the existence of such meanings-in-common contend with the re-cast governmental meanings in the production of that particular being-ness in common termed the 'volunteer'.

Furthermore, they contend within the very universalising space of appearance constructed by the state.

I: so you work here at XXXX [the anti-poverty programme]?
J1:   I'm not a worker—I'm a volunteer.

---

[3] Indeed in this article, they tend to function as cause and effect: they volunteer because they are disadvantaged and they're disadvantaged because they volunteer.

J1 is saying that volunteering provides her with a stake in the actions and containment which dictate the terms through which commonality is to be decided within the space of appearance of the project.

We believe that the study of this space and the investigation of the inter-relationality of variant meanings-in-common are productive of far more subtle outcomes than simplistic linkages of policy might suggest.

It may help explain, for instance, the total failure of the Big Society project itself (Guardian 20 January 2015).

Now, let us examine how these different interpretations of volunteering work themselves out within the space of appearance provided by the office of the anti-poverty programme.

The Office Full of Volunteers

What is immediately apparent is that the spaces of appearance in this office contains an ongoing, interactive, albeit largely silent, question concerning the terms for the construction of being-ness held in common.

The question of how to achieve commonality between these adjacent meanings-in-common constitutes the unspoken pre-occupation among all elements within the community intervention office on the estate.

There are three forms of being-ness existing within the office at any one time. All three demand action and meaning-in-common. The ill-fit between these modes ultimately underlies the perceived failure of the office.

These three modes are as follows:

The professional. Employed by the national funder, runs an office where every piece of furniture is provided by the funder, has ultimate say on all official matters, health and safety procedure, budgetary and mission statements, and responsible for the day-to-day running of all the events occurring within the space. This particular professional was a veteran of many schemes. In the interviews this particular professional veered between several different positions: one is an understanding of the estate's issues, one blaming them for the limitations of the project's impact, claiming the volunteers weren't up to scratch, and one lamenting the terms under which the project's work was enacted and judged.

The volunteer. The office had a strong core of volunteers. All women. Some had social work degrees or were in the process of achieving them. All of them were from the estate. Most of them had worked in various projects previously on the estate, particularly one project they'd helped run without professionals.

The workplace trainees. In the period we worked with the intervention project, approximately seven workplace trainees completed seven-week placements. Occasionally, there were two doing placements simultaneously. All of them were young women somewhere between 20 and 25 in age. They worked from 9 am to 3 pm.

Workplace trainees are specifically tasked with doing courses, learning skills, gaining work experience and accreditation, filling out their CV and making them more employable. In this space of appearance, this training focussed on office duties, answering the phone, passing on enquiries and manning the front desk reception.

It should be remembered, though it is often overlooked, that workplace trainees are not volunteers. They are people being paid in kind, rather than wages; they are being instructed, assessed and ultimately validated.

Thus, the terms of their being-ness exhibit significant difference from that of either the volunteer or the professional. Perhaps that is why within this space of appearance, workplace trainees often appeared slightly nervous and withdrawn.

Most of all, of course, they are utterly dependent on government; by whom, much is requested but little appears to be returned, at least not in this office, by way of face-to-face training or meaningful qualification. It was noticeable that work trainees did not as a rule frequent the office once their placements had expired.[4]

Through all of this, the volunteers ran the office. They ran the after-school clubs, the trips, the credit union and the coffee mornings, all of which brought people into the office. Yet even as they did this, their

---

[4] These three distinct meanings in common creative of social being-ness from their inter-relationality, all confirms, implicitly or explicitly, the subsuming of older notions of volunteering into the current emphasis on volunteering as an aspect of labour market policy (Baines and Hardrill 2008, op cit).

suggestions and offered information were ignored. Silent work was all that was expected from them—obedience, as if they were workplace trainees.

Ramifications of the Circulation of These Divergent Meanings-in-Common

These opposing positions, where, on the one hand, the volunteers felt underutilised, while professionals perceived volunteers as being incapable of providing the help required, clearly had ramifications within the office as a space of appearance.

The volunteers felt dispensable, exploited and excluded, while the staff felt overwhelmed. As one respondent observed, the office was replete with undercurrents of resentment and boredom. The volunteers felt they were accorded neither respect nor input as people who could assist, and the trainees simply got bored, sitting at the front desk or making cups of tea. 'All while the problems the volunteers wanted addressed, never got addressed.'

The results of this are clear in the interviews, which present frequent complaints from volunteers concerned with both the lack of things to do and the terms under which the work was given and performed.

Many volunteers complained privately to us that all they did was 'meet and greet' and make cups of tea. Others mentioned the fact that their suggestions were ignored. One volunteer, decrying this situation, claimed that the professionals 'didn't trust anyone' and that it was 'their way or the highway'. She also repeated the claims of others' that local volunteers from the estate wanted to do something about the long-standing problems on the estate: drug issues, neglect issues and the domestic violence rates, but that the government agency viewed the estate as deficient and by extension viewed the local volunteers from the estate in the same light. This respondent and others also commented frequently that the national government agency was too hidebound by regulation and that the project weren't allowed to tackle these issues because suggestions did not conform to national targets and procedures.

One long-standing volunteer on her own volition drew up a manual outlining what responsibilities and tasks each person was to perform in the office. 'But of course', as she reported to us, 'it was never bloody used was it'. This particular volunteer was a long-standing attendee who had been working in the office for three or four years. She described the entire process as 'very frustrating', 'like hitting your head against a brick wall', and also reported that she only continued because she needed somewhere to go once she retired.

We have seen how issues arose between volunteers and the professionals concerning the giving of advice. Many volunteers from that period stressed their own experience to us in interviews and stressed it again if they departed from the official script.

As one said:

I took her into the room you know for a couple hours…. Talking to her…I got into trouble for that…… she [the community professional] said I should have passed her on. Times it got difficult. Someone had a moan but this girl was someone I knew … and she needed someone she knew.

In addition to these issues of personal reactions, during our observation of the office, one thing that also became apparent was the large number of what we came to call 'micro-dramas': flare-ups between people within the office, often arising from minor events: a word spoken out of place, a tone of voice, some perceived slight.

Often the volunteer in question would then absent herself or himself from the office for a period—sometimes prolonged, sometimes brief. The staff saw these incidents as common features of this kind of programme. They spoke about the difficulty of achieving commonality and about the lack of involvement by the volunteers in any sort of project which might unite them in some overarching cause, without apparently seeing the irony that the volunteers had an overriding cause: their estate; the issue was that it wasn't recognised or acknowledged.

Micro-dramas of this sort further undermined the morale, simply because the process was so ongoing. Additionally, of course they exhausted the energy of the professional office manager who was forever putting out grassfires. No wonder that, in our interviews, the office professionals tended to turn the failure to make substantial project progress back onto the people of the estate.

We have got volunteers who need training and is that our job to provide volunteering opportunities? I don't think maybe the volunteering is very productive and maybe that needs looking at. There is a massive difference in the voluntary sector in the county and up here [on the estate] a huge difference.

Nor is this tension specific to this office. Other investigations have also observed tension between paid and unpaid workers (Baines and Handrill 2008). One reason often cited for this (ibid) is the supposedly unreliable nature of volunteers. However, notions of unreliability can only arise where the volunteers are expected to perform like workers; where, in short, volunteering is dictated and hierarchical, rather than co-operative and expressed in terms of a co-operative commonality; where volunteers are resources, not a form of communal being-ness in common.

One of the strongest props of governance underlying the construction of this space of appearance, a space where volunteers and local knowledge is not even recognised, is the notion of deficiency.

According to this approach, community is deficient; it is lacking and it is the job of intervention to restore this lack. In this formulation, there is no room for credible local knowledge, alternative channels of intervention or local input of any sort. Indeed, inherent within this mode of thinking is the barely concealed notion that there is no such thing as community or communal being-ness present at all.

All of this becomes apparent through studying the space of appearance constructed within the office of the anti-poverty programme.

What was the volunteer who tried to standardise project procedure within the office, and went to a lot of effort to do so, requesting? If it wasn't for her being-ness to be ascribed with commonality, something ultimately in her action was denied.[5]

---

[5] Something we should bear in mind before we rush to inscribe this as 'resistance' or even 'oppositional' in any simple sense.

This, inter-relation between normal governmental and informal community meanings and the manner in which governmentality attempts to formalise the creation of being-ness in common, undoubtedly constrains the operation of both state and the volunteers: what the estate could provide the state does not recognise or want, and what the state requires the communal being-ness does not want to give.

N8, an energetic twentyish male, summed it all up quite succinctly:

I: *If you were going to try and re-build the community here, to bring it up to different levels, what would be some of the things you would think about doing?*
N: *Engagement.*
I: *Engagement how?*
N: *Engagement through utilising people who are from the community, like myself, who come from big families, don't need to make those contacts, don't have that element where they have to build a relationship, we've already got it, and continuous support, don't just tick the boxes for outcomes, have ones that are open, my project is finished, but I still keep in contact, like I work and spend my time helping out, I don't get paid for it, but that's not what I'm about, I want to see my community thrive, and you have got to start with the basics like, you know, if you could do something better it would be to look at people's living standards, actually go into their homes, and help them improve like their erm, you know, their hygiene in the home, things like that, help them, you know, go from the chaotic way that they live, going from one, you know, situation to another, where it's a complete nightmare, start taking that out of the equation, help them to look at, life coach them basically.*
I: *Isn't that the job that the council, and the social workers, try and do?*
N: *Yea, yea, like they try to do things like that, but yea, they are so bound by their policies, and operating systems which, in my view, doesn't allow you to actually do those type of things, they come in, they lay the law down, they say you have got to do this, you have got to do that, oh, we will send someone to help you, but they don't look at like the finer points of why exactly is this situation the way it is, spend some time there, like*

spend a long period of time there if it needs it, because it's going to cut down on costs in the future, and help people, like actually start living their lives in a way that's going to help them have better prospects.

N8's proposals build on what is there already: personal contact, existing knowledge, existing links; in short, all the elements of existing communal being-ness. It is, as N8 notes, both a cheaper option and a more efficient one. It is also of course more an action of mutual aid, rather than the action of governmentality.

But the fact is that, at the funder's insistence, volunteers must work through organisations of this sort—the idea contained in the 'Big Society' paper—which means effectively that funding is unavailable for any form of communal enhancement outside these channels.

Further, the deficiency model stresses individuality, issues of health and education. It is results driven, and, low as the targets are, they are routinely missed. Yet these are the measures for assessing the success, failure or need of the community. One project finishes and routinely another comes along, with equally unrealistic project aims, once again couched in the deficiency framework and managerial language of the previous one.

In regard to the repetitive failure to achieve these targets, even the county council's future planning document mentioned earlier is termed 'No one left *further* behind'.

The deficiency theory is most prominent in social capital accounts and while it might justify the space of appearance constructed by governance, it does so by disqualifying and pathologising communal meanings and modes of communal being-ness.

We saw how within two months of the county umbrella organisation assuming control of the estate facility, after the demise of the anti-poverty intervention, the volunteers literally all left and the office became impossible to keep open. Ideas and suggestions were proposed by the volunteers. This is not deficiency; this is presence.

What also becomes clear from this whole account is that the meanings-in-common particular to the estate present a coherent notion of volunteering at odds with that of the state.

Further, the estate's notion of volunteering is itself part of a coherent meaning-in-common that understands how to improve the estate, based upon modes of sociality and inter-relationality the volunteers themselves understand as constituting the communal being-ness of the estate.

The issue is that none of them were listened to or valued for this knowledge or this understanding.

This paternalistic refusal to engage directly with residents of this estate even as volunteers is counter-productive for the umbrella organisation itself. It denies the organisation access to knowledges which could assist their task. It increases the likelihood of financial waste simply because the real issues are rarely targeted. Finally, it leaves a legacy of distrust and apathy which makes future interventions much more difficult. Moreover, as we shall now see, the entire procedure is an unnecessary duplication of something already present.

Existing Volunteer Organisations and Activities in Market-Town

In Chapter 3, we described the route running from the estate into the town. At the bottom of this track, after one has crossed the car park, as one stands at the pedestrian lights ready to enter the shopping precinct, there is a long, narrow, unprepossessing grey fibro hut with a small garden and a flagpole at the front.

This hut was built after the war with materials donated by local businesses, and for 50 years it has been the hall of the Market-Town pensioners' organisation, an entirely voluntary, unaffiliated organisation run by a volunteer committee of eight or nine people for the entire period of its existence.

Here, every Tuesday, for the past 12 years, RP2, now an 85-year-old man born and bred in Market-Town, has run a seniors' lunch—or to be precise-he and his wife and the eight or nine members of the committee have, for they all have been as much a part of it as he has.

Every year since I started I say I'm going to stop but we can't find someone else to run it.

RP2 was asked to take over running of this hall by the previous committee chairman. As he records it, his wife had been working on the committee for two years before that. He took it over because he was free and retired.

Every Tuesday for over 50 years, the entirely unaffiliated, unregistered pensioners' organisation has offered lunch for pensioners. Typically over RP2's 12-year period, the hall, which holds 60 or 70 people seated, has been full for every lunch: 'not a chair left,' said RP2. The lunch itself was never free but it was cheap, cheaper than in town, and all the money gathered went into bonds, collected and purchased by the committee with the ultimate aim of sustaining the service. Once a month every second Friday they had a speaker and an afternoon tea, which was free and every third Wednesday they ran a trip either to some gardens or to a film or the seaside in summer. In addition, they provided every Christmas a free dinner, free entertainment and a free gift for everyone who attended. All these activities were completely self-financed and, to repeat, had been going on for over 50 years.

At no stage, according to RP2, had the council ever 'really helped'. Even when the hall was burgled, they fixed the front door themselves, as well as refitting the kitchen to achieve a 5* hygiene rating and attaching guide rails for the bathrooms. Indeed, RP2 described the relationship with the council as 'non-existent'.

What is important to emphasise for the purpose of this argument is that this facility was extremely popular. Drawing people equally from the town, the estate and from outlying villages, it was entirely initiated and financed by local volunteers who maintained and improved the facility and the service over that period.

If there was ever an example of the value of self-help and self-empowerment, this pensioners' organisation represents the reality of how volunteering can help sustain and enhance communal life.

Within the space of appearance constituted by the hall, the attendance of the committee serves to activate the empowerment of everyone else. The care and diligence of RP2 and his wife in spending one afternoon a week tending the garden, their capacity for self-help, the stability and transparency with which their affairs were ordered, in turn created a solid foundation for the continuation of the services they provided. There are many examples of this sort of volunteering ethos throughout Market-Town, but for continuity and stability over a remarkable length of time, this stood out for us as an example of what volunteering can achieve when the space of appearance is relatively uncluttered by regulation or non-government organisational self-interest and vanity.

Given that the Cabinet paper describing the Big Society project stated that volunteering should work under the remit of the given power of competence ascribed to local councils, it is salutary to consider what happened when the Market-Town Pensioners' organisation was disbanded in January 2015.

As described by RP2, the basic problem was they had all got old together. Now, when he wanted to stop, touching 85 as he was, there was simply no one left capable of running it. One would think that the town council would welcome the opportunity to assist in the maintenance of such a long-standing project, one which had provided an important service to older citizens and which had cost the council nothing.

What actually happened was the council took back the site and immediately listed it with a local agent asking £10,000 a year for rent, while also actively seeking buyers.

How were they able to do this? According to RP2, he had always believed that the organisation owned the site. However, at some point in the 1990s, the council turned up with papers showing that during the 1960s two of the trustees had signed control of the site over to the council. RP2 tried to discover how this had occurred, but by then the two trustees, whose names were on the deed, were deceased and there was no record of any discussion of this in the organisation minutes from the period. In short, the town council, never having contributed a penny in any form to this organisation or their facilities, which were built using donated materials from local companies, now owned a resource and a commercially valuable piece of land. Thus, a 60-year-old facility containing the input of many volunteers was now a council resource to be disposed of, perhaps to help fund the planned new colour palette for the main shopping street. Indeed, it was reported to us that a group in the town had indeed offered to continue the Tuesday lunches, but the town council had demanded a non-negotiable fee of a £100 per lunchtime, making it impossible.

Nor is this the only instance described to us where the blurring of lines had resulted in money gathered by volunteers, apparently 'disappearing' into council coffers. In any case, in the particular context of the Pensioners' organisation, it simply meant that RP2 cashed in the bonds the organisation had saved and distributed £500 per person among the volunteers and lunchtime regulars.

The great irony of all of this is that throughout Market-Town, there are countless volunteers expressing this sense of mutual aid, among all sectors of the population and all areas of the town. We saw in Chap. 3, how the community association organised trips for people from the estate and how they were all volunteers, in Chap. 6, how people served on housing associations for many years and in Chap. 4, we mentioned the woman and her friends who volunteered to run street parties and who, with others, redeemed a garden area at the end of the main street. These are just some examples.

In the two and half years we were investigating life in Market-Town, we found this sort of activity throughout the town. Many groups raised substantial amounts of money for the improvement of the main park, developing flowerbeds and erecting scented gardens in neglected areas of the park.

Failure of the Big Society and Its Notion of Volunteering

Taking the 'Big Society' blue print as an example, we can see how the government assumes that it is the only source of any social action; it is the one to make it happen —the active agent. In fact as we saw this claim is redundant, because it is already happening.

What seems to underlie this refusal of the government to recognise their own limitations and indeed to recognise already existing occurrences of 'volunteering' is a refusal to acknowledge sources of social power other than their own.

On 20 January 2015, the Civil Exchange, 'a think tank that exists to help government and the voluntary sector work better together', published its final audit of the Big Society initiative. The basic claim of the report is that the 'Big Society has failed to deliver against its original goals.' It concludes that 'attempts to create more social action, to empower communities and to open up public services, …have not worked (ibid)' and the Big Society 'leaves the voluntary sector a key source of support for disadvantaged groups and route to understanding their needs—not strengthened but weakened' (ibid).

Tellingly, the report claims volunteer numbers had failed to increase, while social action has been largely concentrated in more affluent areas and levels of disenchantment with government have actually increased.

While we completely support this damning of the failure of the Big Society as a programme, nevertheless, the problem remains that communities are still positioned as passive receivers of government help. The report fails to locate these communities and their expressed needs at the forefront of their analysis, and they continue to believe in concepts like 'civil society' and the willingness of government to devolve or empower. In short, they remain welded to the notion that only certain groups, state-recognised groupings, must 'represent' community and not the community residents themselves.

Our research has found that at least in the context of the estate, residents do have a clear idea of what is needed and how they can provide it. It is also clear they are armed with a strong desire to provide this help for each other on a voluntary basis.

We could argue that successive governments have failed to recognise this because they are quite unwilling politically to recognise or allow estate residents the capacity to act positively in their own communities and for this independent action by communities, to be supported financially and strategically.

These final examples will show not only that this is impossible for government to consider as an action, but that one of the biggest existing constraints upon such real communal participation is indeed the very forces of governmentality which claim to speak for the community and claim they seek to assist the community.

Two slightly different examples from Market-Town will help us understand our claim.

The first one concerns how, on their own volition, members of the community association mentioned in Chap. 2 established a food kitchen in the local leisure centre. It was entirely staffed by volunteers and served food to a variety of people: council workers, pensioners and people from the estate. All the food was donated by local businesses and picked up beforehand by volunteers. After running successfully for a couple of months it took on some excluded school students from the truancy centre who did health and safety certificates and used the facilities to learn kitchen skills intended to lead to various certifications. After six months, the local council demanded £120 per week from the group, which, lacking any resources, was simply unable to pay. The inevitable result was the closure of the facility. The town council has also refused to run any local courses that would allow locals to gains accreditation for the hospitality industry or to ensure that local developments like supermarkets employ local people.

The second example concerns an unused building, formerly a disused school, located in the town itself. A group from the street where the disused facility stood, began a campaign to turn it into a neighbourhood 'drop-in centre'. This campaign took five years. It was a long, exhausting endeavour on the part of this group. From the first, the town and county council operated as a blocking agent for the conversion. Finally, after five years of intense lobbying the council agreed to provide the disused site as what they referred to as a community centre. However, to achieve even this step, the organisation was forced by the council to run the centre as a commercial enterprise, if they wanted to use the building at all. This council imposed status, virtually guaranteed limited usage and a lack of wide participation, particularly from people on the estate. One result of this enforced commercial status is that previous plans to run a cafe and provide computer access for job seekers now appear to be shelved. While the website for the facility lists various activities: a knitting club, Friday night and Friday morning clubs, a toddlers club, a Lego club, yoga and various courses run by private individuals, these are the sorts of events which severely limit the use of the building for the entire town. None of this is the fault of the community group who began with a much wider and more inclusive vision where the facility would be an asset for the entire town. Its current situation is clearly an outcome of the restrictions placed upon it by the town and county councils.

However, this consideration did not impair the council in making public claims in their future planning document that use of this disused site represented a great achievement and continued proof of their willingness to engage in 'community cohesion'.

Both these examples present instances of existing and potential spaces of appearance constructed by people acting in common. In both cases the town and county councils either destroyed or severely constrained the possibilities created by this action in common.

In the first example, this effectively forced the closure of one site; in the second, it severely constrained the operations to the point where the original aims were effectively undermined. The volunteers, who to repeat, had constructed these sites from their own efforts, as an attempt to enhance the wider communal being-ness of the town, were thus denied the opportunity to develop communal being-ness by the very same forces who constantly claim to want to enhance communal cohesion.

What the sum of our data convincingly shows is that it is not communal being-ness which presents the real obstacle to enhance and empower communities, but rather government and its various so-called non-governmental arms. It is *they* who have to learn to listen rather than impose; they who have to work as equals in the process rather than demanding the space of appearance be crowded and closed with pre-emptively imposed meanings derived from their web of relations.

For real progress to occur, this mindset imposed by government, through the guise of its myriad of organisations, needs to respect the sociality and the being-ness in common that creates these spaces of appearance, stay out of the way, and stop imposing their household ideas upon the communal being-ness. Something almost impossible to imagine ever happening.

Conclusion

In this chapter, we have been at pains to point out that the technologies of governance described by Foucault nearly half a century ago do not simply operate to produce subjects as though there were no other input. By attempting to understand the practices of governmentality as one aspect among others within the web of relations, we began to understand that being-ness is constituted multiply, with practices of governmentality operating to define volunteering set against understandings of volunteering that come from within a different space of appearance. Thus, the volunteer is not simply a figure created within the recent government interventions. That such a figure exists is strongly demonstrated within the examples we have given. But equally, we have demonstrated that the meanings generated to define the volunteer sit in relation to other practices in which volunteering exists as a form of self-help. What the specific analysis of examples allows us to see is the contestation in action. Thus, when we argue that community can be understood as the production of communal being-ness through meanings-in-common, we have attempted to point out that the meanings produced through governmentality are meanings which sit amongst others and are not the sole basis on which the modern individual is formed. That governmentality attempts to produce this individual is not in doubt. But to simply see other forms of being-ness as resistance is both to deny these other forms veracity and to, indeed, mimic and unintentionally support the claims of governmentality to be the exclusive source for the construction of being-ness in common. While, as we have shown, the estate volunteers do resist the meanings implied by the community workers, they do so because they exist within a space of appearance defined first and foremost by other meanings-in-common. In this sense then, governmentality, or what we could call the state, exists less as a monolith and more as one among an inter-related set of meanings.

Conversely, this analytic begins with communal being-ness as the source of all subjectivity. It offers a de-centralised location where subjectivities are both constructed outside of the state/individual axis or modes of governmentality and can be changed and altered outside of that axis. It sees the state and the individual as outcomes of communal being-ness and sociality itself (King P. op cit, p. 182). Even spaces of appearance as clogged with regulation and containment as some we have investigated here, are not in any way productive of a single subjectivity as an exclusive outcome of state input.

We hope what this chapter has demonstrated is not just that communal meanings and the meanings of governmentality are not identical but that using the notions of being and meaning-in-common as well as derived notions, such as meanings-in-common, allow us a much more nuanced view of the inter-relations in which governmentality exists as one meaning-in-common within the multiplicity of meanings-in-common that is the web of relations.

Bibliography

Baines, S., & Hardill, I. (2008). 'At least I can do something': The work of volunteering in a community beset by worklessness. *Social Policy and Society, 7*, 307–317. doi:10.1017/S1474746408004284.

Baines, S., Sue, H., & Robon, W. (2011, July). Introduction: Remixing the economy of welfare? Changing: Roles and relationships between the state and the voluntary and community sector. *Social Policy and Society, 10*(03), 337–339 (Published online: 01 June 2011).

Evers, H.-D. (2003). Transition towards a knowledge society: Malaysia and Indonesia in comparative perspective. *Comparative Sociology, 2*(2), 355–373.

Milligan, Christine; Fyfe, Nicholas R (2004) Putting the voluntary sector in its place: geographical perspectives on voluntary activity and social welfare in Glasgow. Journal of Social Policy, 33(1), 01.2004, p. 73–93. https://www.gov.uk/government/publications/building-the-big-society 2010

Portes, A. (1998). Social capital: Its origins and applications in modern sociology. *Annual Review of Sociology, 24*, 1–24.

Putnam, R. D., Leonardi, R., & Nanetti, R. (1993). *Making democracy work*. Princeton: Princeton University Press.

Putnam, R. (2000). *Bowling alone: The collapse and revival of the American community*. New York: Simon & Schuster.

Roberts, J. M., & Devina, F. (2003). The hollowing out of the welfare state and social capital. *Social Policy and Society, 2*(4), 309–318.

Rose, N. (1999). *Powers of freedom*. Cambridge: Cambridge University Press.

Susan Baines and Irene Hardill (2008). 'At Least I Can Do Something': The Work of Volunteering in a Community Beset by Worklessness. Social Policy and Society, 7, pp 307–317 doi:10.1017/S1474746408004284

Studdert, D. (2006). *Conceptualising community: Beyond the state and the individual*. London: Palgrave.

Young, J. (1999). *The exclusively society: Social exclusion, crime and difference in late modernity*. London: Sage.

8

Community Policing

I: *You always felt safe.*
R: *Always safe because there was always ….someone around.*

The previous chapter discussed volunteering, using the communal analytic which the book seeks to develop.

This chapter discusses policing in Market-Town. In particular, we discuss the relationality between the communal being-ness of the estate and the different set of communal meanings actioned as policing. We want to see what state policing looks like from the other end of the telescope, the viewpoint of the estate.

While we are not criminologists, nor do we pretend to understand the entire field, our interest in thinking about crime and the town was piqued by Gordon Hughes' (2007) comment that the key to thinking about policing in new ways is to think about community.

We therefore feel warranted in examining the actions of sociality understood as policing, to see if, through our analytic, we might establish the meanings-in-common and constructive within that action. We begin by examining a mode of policing that would have operated in Market-

© The Author(s) 2016
D. Studdert, V. Walkerdine, *Rethinking Community Research*,
DOI 10.1057/978-1-137-51453-0_8

Town at the time of the heyday of Henry St. This mode of policing was national both in Britain and in the USA (Skogan 1997)

Policing Around Henry St

Pre-1950s' British policing was characterised by the intimate, communally endorsed positioning of the policeman (and it was a man) within the sociality of the communal being-ness, a communal being-ness to which the police adjusted.[1] In that role, it was almost as though (at least according to interviews with residents) the figure could be understood as *the community-controlled* policeman. The police presence maintained itself as an element in the construction of communal being-ness and thus was able to influence that being-ness and the resultant communal meanings it generated.

As a result, linkages developed by the police appear not only to have been generally accepted by the particular communal being-ness, but the presence of the policeman inside the local web of relations helped to stabilise communal being, shaping it through the presence and visibility. In this way the local policeman on the beat became a meaning as well as a presence for the containment of action. This inter-linkage is well illustrated here:

> *I remember once pinching apples on the way to school, and I got a clip across the ear off the lady that owned the apples and I just gets to school and the policeman was there. I gets a cut across my legs, and of course you only wore shorts in them days. So I goes home and granddad seen it, the marks on my legs and so I had two cuts then off granddad with his belt. One for pinching the apples and one for telling a lie.*

---

[1] Of course this is not quite how various criminology texts describe the process (Skogan 1997); however, a close reading of their descriptions of this style of policing shows that from another perspective this is a fair description. One of the issues we have noticed in the criminology texts we have read is that everything is always described from the viewpoint of the police, even if they claim otherwise.

The manner in which the particular policeman—and policemen were consistently recalled and named in these interviews—was embedded in the community can be deduced from this account about one such policeman:

> *Yeah, it used to be, 'cause Sergeant Grant used to live in there and his son was apprenticed with me down at Smiths and we spent a lot of time up there in the Police Station with him. Always building radios or something and his father, sergeant, he'd give us a few rollockings and stuff. His radio's blaring. We reckoned we could hear it down in the bus station. He'd come up there, he used to give us a lecture. Ay, Sergeant Grant. Then he retired. He was gateman down at Smiths for a long time.*

It appears, from these examples, that the police from that era enforced authority, not legality. Often this was, as in the first example, familial authority. Of course, this was aided by homogenous communities and police who were racially the same as the community they served and of course it concealed, just as present practices conceal, examples and incidents of widespread domestic and sexual abuse, as well as the frequent use of corporal punishment. We do not want to ignore these issues, but neither should we allow them to distract our discussion from the main point we wish to make. Policing was driven by an informal code of interaction between police and community and characterised by the intimate, communally-endorsed positioning of the police within the sociality of the communal being-ness, a communal being-ness to which the police adjusted. In that role, as almost *the community-controlled* policeman, the police presence maintained itself as an element in the construction of being-ness and thus was able to influence that being-ness and the resultant communal meanings it generated.

Moreover, people knew where the boundaries were, and these boundaries were crucial to the containment of their communal being-ness by providing that which was commonly known and enacted in common.[2]

---

[2] The function of boundaries as a form of containment is primarily a discourse which comes from a psychoanalytic literature, but, for example, see Guattari's reference to the work of Daniel Stern, to whom repeated rituals in child care provides an ontological security that allows a subject to emerge.

Of course, if punishment is perceived as excessive or cruel, then this was not the case, but as the following quote makes clear, these boundaries were agreed and were perceived as fair and, indeed, were also subject to their own informal checks and balances within the sociality of the surrounding communal being-ness.

R:　*And also there was a big sense of natural justice, a wonderful sense. I can remember my grandmother saying if you clipped a child around the ear for nothing, you'd get one back.*
I:　*And what happened if you clipped them around the ear for something they had done?*
R:　*Oh, that was fine, that was fine.*

The other theme that dominated policing in that period is intimacy; intimacy of the police and the communal being-ness within their common spaces of appearance and their common actions of sociality. We have seen some examples of this already, but this example reveals it in terms of punishment.

R:　*Yes, many a times a policeman used to take his cape off and whip you with it, like, you know, and it stung.*
　　That happened to you then, did it?
R:　*Oh yes, yes.*

In all the instances offered by respondents, the sociality between the policeman (a person) and the community was mutually constituting and constructive of an entwined commonality; the communal was the public and the police—there were meanings held in common shared between the policeman who beat the boy and the grandfather who did likewise in upholding familial authority, for better or for worse.

Of course, this took place within a town where, as we saw in Chapter 6, the working population lived in the centre of town, lived very close to each other and where work, if not well paid, was nonetheless plentiful. All of these elements functioned to maintain a strong sense of communal being-ness through sociality and commonality of particular being-ness.

While we do not wish to offer a nostalgic view of this period, which no doubt contained myriad problems and issues, it is important to stress that the accounts given to us present the police as part of the reinforcement of a containing authority. The space of appearance where this being-ness in common was constructed was relatively regular and understood. Further, within this space of appearance, policing functioned as one element of containment supportive of other modes of containment and did so in a relatively regularised manner, in an atmosphere that some commentators still like to characterise as stifling conformity. We might suggest that such a designation misses the point. As Walkerdine (2010) and Walkerdine and Jimenez (2012) argued, when conditions for a community are continually unstable, rigid kinds of rules as containment help to keep fear away by providing what Bick (1968) called a 'second skin', a rigid sets of rules used to maintain commonality in the face of what can be experienced as potentially annihilating.

The estate in contrast was, from the very first, characterised by disruption of the containers of safety and the breaking of this 'second skin'. First, the various familiar social groupings of Henry Street were, as we saw in Chap. 6, broken up by relocation. Secondly, the houses were of a modern sort, which curtailed intimacy and inter-relationality and through that communal being-ness and protective communal oversight of each other. Finally, the period after 1980 was characterised by increased economic insecurity coupled with the influx of drugs and the issues attendant upon that.

At the same time, the place of policing within that web of relations has become increasingly abstract and removed from the immediate sociality of the estate's space of appearance and communal being-ness. As technologies have become more determining of police practice (Skogan 1997), the police have increasingly become, not so much embedded in the communal being-ness, but more overlooking it, operating from a much more removed perspective.

In this regard, nothing illustrates the gap between police understanding of their contemporary role and the common understanding felt by the communal being-ness they are tasked to protect, more than the notion that this abstraction has improved policing, made it more transparent and that notions like 'community policing' have embedded the police more firmly into the community. Or, as one academic put it, 'the fit between the police and community is now better than ever (Garland, 2000, p. 126).'

Our interviews on the estate do not support this view. They are full of concerns over safety and ontological security. For the estate, the preservation of their most precious resource, the unity generated by the own communal being-ness, has become increasingly problematic.

Partially, this fear is a 'rational response' to the decline in police presence on the estate itself.

I: *Do you ever see them walking around the estate?*

R: *Well, if you're lucky, you might see one now and again, you know, sometimes you see a police officer, and a PCSO [**police community support officer: they have limited legal power**], I also know inspectors, Inspector Garfield and we've had a few words now and again like, because they dedicated a PCSO now for every area.*

I: *Yea.*

R: *So, it's good like, you know, you have got one for every area, but then you get a Friday, Saturday and Sunday, and they take them off then, and they take them into town, you know, because that's when we have trouble in Market-Town.*

Another respondent is of much the same opinion, expressed in an even more holistic and desperate form, which might indicate how defenceless he feels:

Well if anything goes wrong in Market-Town, they call the police and it takes the police half an hour to get there 'cause they've got to come from [nearby town]. Well that's not the right way to keep the law, is it? You know, it's ridiculous. But this government's been getting rid of policemen, been getting rid of the Army, the Navy. How are we supposed to defend ourselves?

In its own way, an even more telling example is the humorous response of one man when asked, if he had trouble getting policemen:

No, we know Daisy across the road. 'Course she's still got a job. Opposite the station. So we want to get in touch with the police or anything, we ring Daisy across the road.

In any case whatever their presence or absence the police are characteristically perceived as not particularly helpful in the protection of either body or possessions.

I: *Erm, and in general, if you went to the police and reported some sort of, you know, say your mate who got his car wheels stolen, did he go to the police and report it?*
R: *Yea.*
I: *What did they do?*
R: *Nothing, just took his name and number, and they have got the car registration, but they didn't do nothing else after that.*
I: *And, is that common?*
R: *It's common around here.*

But disenchantment with the level of policing is only one element within the feeling of lack of safety. For this problematic police presence runs parallel with safety fears arising from changes in the social world of the estate itself.

This decline in the simple experience of 'feeling safe' stems directly from the increasing difficulties of social being-ness to construct itself *in common* and therefore maintain its own communal being-ness.

The increasing difficulty of constructing and maintaining a being-ness in common stems directly from the precarious existence of many of the estate residents; work is precarious; benefits are precarious; health and resources are precarious, space is precarious, homes are precarious.

And most precarious of all, the biggest most apparent threat to this communal commonality, this being-in-common-with-each-other, is drugs. However, even drugs are only one of an ongoing parade of events in what sometimes feels like a paper thin skin, holding together the communal being-ness of the estate. These are what we shall briefly describe now—the threats to the estate's being in common.

Threats to Communal Safety

Drugs

The estate itself, as many reported, contains an ongoing and 'enormous' heroin problem. When asked, one respondent replied in terms mirrored by many others:

> *Oh yeah massive. Heaps are on it. Half the time you wouldn't know it. You see mums like, with their strollers and they look normal, but they're completely hooked.*

Another respondent confirms this:

> *You see young men during the day just walking round zombied out, clearly out of their heads on smack. Not all the time but a lot, frequently.*

For the communal being-ness of the estate, immediate and concrete contact with drugs fills every part of their life as well as many, many instances of routine sociality; nor does it appear to be going away anytime soon. This apparently constant presence, to which the communal being-ness of the estate is forced to adapt, is constructive of a sociality of resignation, hostility, toleration and coping. The sociality being actioned in these circumstances is direct and intimate and its meanings-in-common constitute a fundamental knowledge in the lives of virtually everyone on the estate.

> *Yea, there is a lot of druggies around this place.*

Another respondent, without judgement, offers this appraisal:

> *I see a lot of kids just roaming the street, and stuff like that, from the sort of rough families, but it's no different to what their parents done ... for those other youngsters that you see on the streets, they start bothering with the older kids, the older kids have already started smoking dope.*

Many accounts confirm this constant presence. The phrase that recurred regularly through the interviews, in various tones from resignation to passionate dislike was the phrase: *you never know what they'll do when they're on it. They don't care.*

This phrase speaks precisely about the perceived threat to commonality in a very concrete way. It evokes the ontological terror of not being able to construct being-ness in common from any of the things that surround you. Given the economic web in which the estate is contained, communal being-ness is its greatest resource for simply getting by.

Of course, an ongoing situation like this is also played out within families, family tragedies: tragedies of betrayal and expulsion all taking place in the most intimate circumstances.

J1, a respondent we have met before, says,

It does sometimes, because I have got one son who is really good, and I have got one son who has gone off the rails, and he won't listen, and unfortunately two years ago I had no choice but to throw him out.

He took something which was very sentimental to me, and he sold it, and I wasn't happy, and I couldn't live like that, but I mean I had to throw him out, but while he was there my house was targeted twice. I had graffiti drawn all over the outside of my wall, paint bombs as it's called.

J1's house has been attacked twice, something she attributes to the behaviour of her errant son while he lived with her. So the issue of drugs affects everyone. Simply by involving herself in the lives of her family, J1 places herself in a position where she is involved in disputes typically engrained within the drug culture. Moreover, when sons steal from mothers, the drug issue brings crime into the home, and threatens the terms for the creation of social being-ness in its most familiar form; undermining the sense of commonality in its most intimate terrain.

'Criminal Families' and Geography

This issue of the safety of immediate space of appearance is also present in an interview conducted with another woman on the estate. Here, the safety of commonality is disrupted by both geography and the presence of other social groupings which, if not hostile, have to be carefully considered before even the most basic action is attempted.

Once again, one element in this is a simple one, relating to the spatial organisation of the estate itself. We spoke in Chap. 3 of how the estate lacked basic services, particularly shops. It is a large, spread-out estate that almost circles one side of the town, and yet within it there are only two shops: a butcher and an off-licence, selling basic food goods, coupled with another one down the hill on the edge of the estate. This is an observation central to grasping the significance of the next example concerning personal safety and why the spatial structure of the estate plays a strong role in the lack of communal safety that we are examining.

Our respondent described the everyday dilemmas created by the estate's spatial organisation. She has no car.

I: *And in general on this estate, do you think it is a safe place?*
R: *Where I live it's safe.*
I: *Right.*
R: *On the other side, which well, as I said isn't far from me, it is not so safe.*
I: *And which part is that?*
J1:   *That's Deephollow.*
I: *so you wouldn't walk over there by yourself?*
J1:   *I would, but I am very uneasy when I do walk over there. I try not to use the shop over there if I can.*
I: *Right is there only one shop in that area?*
J1:   *Yea, yes there is, yea.*
I: *And why do you feel not so safe in that area?*
R1:   *Not stereotyping, but there is families over there who seem to think they own the estate, sort of like the attitude this is the west side, their side, and it is sort of like a bit of a gang, if you know what I mean, and they are always outside the shop, and it is such a big family if you have an argument with one, you have got the whole family then on your back.*
I: *When you say a big family, there is ten, or twenty of them?*
J1:   *Oh yea, if not more, yea.*
I: *And they are all relatives, they are all related?*

R1: All related, and they all live in the same street, and they can make some
people who, nice people who want to get on with their lives, they can
make their lives misery, and sometimes they do.

These two families were mentioned in almost 75 % of the interviews
as the source of most of the crime in Market-Town, as was the area they
live in, called for purposes of anonymity, 'Deephollow'. Many other confirmed the account of these families provided by the female respondent.

One respondent described these two families as taking part in an
'ongoing' low-level war in which, if provoked, at least in their terms,
gangs of 20 people would turn up on antagonistic doorsteps with baseball
bats, windows would get smashed and very occasionally a shot or two get
fired. These are described in interviews as 'extended families' but they also
include people with what the respondent, called 'drug links'.

The general tenor of all estate respondents when asked about engaging in sociality with either of these extended families from 'Deephollow'
can be summed up as 'a fight with one is a brawl with all'. Of course,
these two families are also containing and expressing their own communal being-ness, which in itself is also an inter-relational response to the
world which encases them. The 'moral' rights and wrongs of this do not
concern us. What we want to stress is, firstly and most importantly, that
the existence of this family complicates the commonality of the estate
and the capacity of the estate to develop being-ness in common for itself.
Within the spread-out geography of the estate, the ability to self-police
the behaviour of this family is severely curtailed, unlike the situation in
Henry Street. Secondly, we want to stress that this is an everyday occurrence, one in which policing has no role except reactively, and then, only
when a crime has been committed.

Nonetheless, it is a terrain that this particular woman and many others traverse on a regular basis. The care that she and many others have
to observe doing this constantly gnaws at their sense of commonality
and their sense of knowing their own community and feeling contained
within its spaces of appearance, meanings-in-common and communal
being-ness. All of this contributes in turn to fears for her own safety. Yet
the lack of shops and her lack of resources mean that occasionally she is

forced to engage with both the area and her own fears concerning these families.

Domestic Violence

We have stated already that domestic violence on the estate is starkly and clearly the highest in the county.

According to many participants, the police, while better than they have traditionally been, in part because of changes to the legal framework, are still reluctant to get involved. Further, when they do get involved, many of the cases are not prosecuted. Thus, while respondents praised the Market-Town Domestic Violence unit, the general feeling was that the police lacked a method for really helping the community address the issue. Domestic violence was something barely discussed in the interviews. Though, as we shall see, one of the residents had a very strong view about what was needed to support the estate in this regard. Domestic violence is not only an action against a person, terrible as that is, it is also a destruction of meanings-in-common concerning the home and safety.

The White Van

This sense of the estate's space of appearance and communal unity as something extremely fragile, constantly requiring diligence and care to maintain even in its most intimate and familiar forms, is also illustrated in this example taken from our field notes.

There it is recorded that on two separate occasions when the researchers were in the anti-poverty office, people came rushing in shouting that an unidentified white van was cruising the estate trying to steal children. People immediately went rushing out around the streets looking for it. In the day following this there was a constant conversation in the office with people sharing the information. Clearly, as they stated, they had little optimism that the police would do anything about it. Indeed, at least four people, including the office professional, told us emphatically that they would not. In the days after, we noticed, according to our field notes, more children in the office.

Moneylending

Illegal moneylending was mentioned many times in interviews: by the professional at the anti-poverty programme and by people who lived on the estate. The sum total of the information gathered was that there was a well-known man—respondents frequently gave his first name. He had been providing money for various families on the estate for 'decades'; he was a late middle-aged man who drove a white luxury saloon and sometimes he drove the people he lent to, down to the post office to cash their cheques. He was on very good terms with these people, particularly the ones he had been 'servicing' over an extended period. Estate respondents interviewed acknowledged the risks of violence if one did not pay, as well as the implications of prolonged indebtedness to such moneylenders. However, without exception, this was coupled with comparisons with the credit card policies of major UK banks, with the dangers of borrowing money legally as well as with the difficulty people on the estate had in borrowing money from high street lenders at all.

The Policy of Government Agencies

What appears to the residents to be the rather careless operational attitude of some government agencies is also a contributing factor in the feelings of insecurity that people on the estate experience. The intensity of their response to certain events is in itself evidence of the manner in which the estate feels itself undermined in its own commonality. The following example comes from 'Deephollow'.

'Deephollow' was commonly described to us as the roughest section of the estate—indeed, the entire town. The name reverberates through Market-Town and throughout our interviews, much in the same way as Henry Street used to; it is certainly a meaning-in-common.

'Deephollow', is an area slightly isolated from the rest of the estate, consisting of about 200 houses existing in seven or eight streets. According to the rough guesses of respondents, about 40 % of inhabitants are in some form of employment. One respondent who lived there for 'about eight years', claims that while he initially refused an offered/allocated house for him and his family in the area, he subsequently was convinced by his partner to locate there and found 'Deephollow' to be 'not as bad as he thought'. He stressed how people 'watched each others' back', a process he supported in his own actions of sociality, as his comment, repeated twice, that 'I made it my business to know everything and everyone' makes clear. Communal 'surveillance', or perhaps neighbourhood watch without state sponsorship, is to this man understood as a necessity.

'Deephollow' is a site of the creation of communal being-ness generating of communal meanings (concerning violence; identity, action) separate from the town's and mutually antagonistic to other communal meanings derived from the same source and operating simultaneously within those seven or eight streets or two hundred houses and one shop.

Here, the state is not the exclusive determiner of modes of containment: it is simply one, among other modes of sociality.

The similarities across time between 'Deephollow' and Henry St are striking. Both are creative of a social being-ness marked by commonality, co-operation and 'crime'. The crime comes usually with attached codes derived primarily from the space of appearance which constituted either Henry Street or 'Deephollow'.

It was present in accounts of Henry Street in comments about adults giving children a clip around the ear if they'd done something that was not ok, and in the follow-up comment that, if indeed, the child had done what was claimed, then nothing further would occur; however, if they hadn't, then the adult would be 'seen to'.

This attitude was repeated almost word for word by the respondent who framed his account of the 'Deephollow' area with his own example, one also concerning children, their behaviour and the behaviour of neighbouring adults. He told a story regarding a confrontation that he was involved in regarding another adult's attitude and behaviour in relation to his son. His exact phrase was 'It was out of order what he [the other man] did.'

This notion of order he's referring to, functions as truth derived from the creation of being-ness and its further creation through meanings-in-common. It entirely stems from the sociality present in both locations. All these elements were also present in Henry Street. One extremely strong element in this communal being-ness, as it was in Henry Street, is family and particularly children.

Returning to our examination of the ongoing threats to commonality, on one occasion a government agency relocated 'Deephollow' a woman who had been convicted of child sex offences. The aggravation felt by the residents of 'Deephollow' in relation to this relocation was further aggravated by the fact that the woman in question was relocated from out of the county and they were not consulted.

I: *Why in Deephollow?*
R: *That's a very good question. I don't understand. It's happening two times in five years you know. Why are they dumping pedos in a place like this, a really tight knit place like Deephollow? They just seem happy to use it as sink hole estate.*

Of course, in a location and a communal being-ness where the place of family and children is so sacrosanct, this relocation presented another challenge to the communal being-ness which, for all its imperfections and incompleteness, remains the major resource for the entire estate. Given the poverty of this area and the fact that, according to the respondent, children typically played in the street, it also presented as a stark undermining of the space of appearance and the community's own notions of itself as a communal being-ness.

Challenging the commonality and agreement required to preserve the space of appearance, and the communal being-ness in such a blatant manner provoked a reaction, and in due course, we examine this reaction. All we need to observe here is that this openly presents other instances where it feels to the residents that their communal being-ness is being undermined by actions from outside the estate, actions threatening of the meanings-in-common sustaining of their communal being-ness.

All these examples give weight to the belief held by estate residents that their communal being-ness is a fragile thing constantly requiring defending and action. Yet, tellingly, this communal being-ness exists at some distance from formal notions of policing.

In the case of the drugs on the estate, the police have an interest of course, but the drug-fuelled events experienced by J1 through the involvement with her addicted son, are not directly a concern of the police.

Nor is the fact that a woman fears walking to the shops, nor the fact that her situation requires her to do so, of interest to the police. Of course, the 'white van' and instances like the moneylending and the domestic violence are matters which breach formal codes of legality. Nonetheless, police activity around these three issues can best be described as spasmodic, if not half-hearted, at least as understood by residents of the estate.

Yet while no breach of formal codes occurs, these examples profoundly affect the communal being-ness of the estate. They also bolster the communal sense that they are under attack and that the things maintaining of their communal being-ness are not being cared for.

The lack of policing means that the commonality required to construct a space of appearance is challenged in all the instances discussed above, either directly or indirectly. This is what accounts for the constant presence of the word 'safety' in interviews. Such instances break down the boundaries within and through which, being-ness in common, communal meanings and, thus, ontological security, are sustained.

That the fears of the estate in this regard are creative of different meanings-in-common is incontrovertible. The police and the community see the same thing with utterly different eyes. Drugs are a good example of this. Estate residents, at least in the interviews, are not concerned at all with questions of decriminalisation or the classification of drugs or even the distinguishing of one drug from another. In relation to drugs, they are concerned entirely with the effect of druggies on their own space of appearance and commonality.

Earlier we spoke briefly of the mode of policing practised previously in the town. It came dressed in 1930s and 1940s clothing. That example showed the authority of the police derived from their policing of communal being-ness. The previous role of the police as figures in authority appears to have been transformed into a completely different set of micro practices containing of a police communal being-ness at odds with, rather than reinforcing of, the communal being-ness of the estate.

Responses to Threats from Estate Communal Being-ness

Given the central place this feeling of vulnerability occupies within the communal being-ness of the estate, it is no surprise that the responses are well developed and, on occasion, dramatic and intense. After all, as we have observed a number of times, for the estate, communal being-ness is its greatest resource.

What we are going to do now is to show how these 'threats drew a response from the estate's communal being-ness, expressed through actions of sociality in common.

In do so, we will hopefully show the estate's commonality of purpose and meaning, the understanding and confidence it has in the value of its own sociality and the determination it shows in sustaining its meanings as different from the police meanings-in-common.

Illegal Moneylending

Returning to the example of moneylending discussed earlier, the distinction between an estate and a professional response is highlighted clearly by citing the responses of both to this practice. The estate resident called the practice 'money borrowing' and recognised the role the lender played in the lives of those who borrow, grasping clearly the necessity for the borrowers, while equally understanding the possible violent consequences of non-payment. The moneylender was viewed as a 'friend' who helped the family.

In contrast, the professional on the anti-poverty programme, while cognisant of the denial of high street credit to people from the estate, nonetheless framed the issue as an illegal deviancy which preyed upon the estate.

Yet, even the professional understands the place of the lender within the informal relations and meanings-in-common of the community, as evidenced by the following reported conversation in the estate office.

So they say "that's xxxx he comes round and gives us money he's got a lovely white car but he's been giving us money for years and years and years". And I say, "well that's illegal, that's money lending that's wrong", erm, "but he's lovely and he's been doing it for years—he's got a relationship with these families for years. He'll give a lift down the Post Office on a Thursday to collect their money".

For the estate residents, the rule of law is much less of an issue here than the relational position of the lender within the space of appearance, whereas for the professional there are abstract categories of legality and morality which take precedence. The disinterest of the estate concerning questions of legality, types of crime, rates of crime, and so on was uniform in the interviews for all topics, including drugs.

Such categories appear to be of little significance in relation to the exigencies of daily life and the place of borrowing, debt and drugs within that web of relations. This example demonstrates clearly how abstract categories of legality and morality assume a figure isolated and rational, for whom such issues are of a higher import than the problem of getting by from day to day. That position makes no sense to the estate.

How the Communal Being-ness Thinks About Domestic Violence: A 'Hand Holding' Community Response

We learned earlier of the serious problem of domestic violence on the estate and how, though improved, the police response was perceived as still inadequate. In this section, we consider the proposed response of one group of volunteers from the anti-poverty programme. This group summed up the general course they would have liked to pursue if they had been allowed to. One group member argued for a more holistic mode driven by education and what she called a 'hand-holding community' approach, which utilised community members from the estate to provide the first engagement with the victims. For her, the hand-holding by other women on the estate would provide a sense of continuity and safety and also an acknowledgement of the ways in which domestic violence took place in very difficult conditions. In this view, the estate community should lead the way and not follow, and police and other professionals should support them as necessary. This view recalls that taken by another volunteer, N8, who we met in Chapter 7 and who wanted estate volunteers to take the lead in supporting estate residents in turning their lives around. Here again, we see how the communal approach is located and sustained inside a shared being-ness in common and not through abstracted categories of legal, illegal, right or wrong.

What is clear from all of this is that the communal being-ness operates as a 'who' capable of solving problems as long as the state supports and assists it. The community does not want to exclude the state. It seeks assistance, but it wants to take the lead and to construct the response in terms of its own communal being-ness and reading of the situation.

Refusal to Work with the Police

In one of our research projects, we had a steering committee composed mostly of local estate residents. At one meeting the two of us proposed inviting various representatives of local government and statutory bodies, including the police, onto the steering group. Initially we had conceived this as a new separate committee to include 'community partners', linking the estate peopled steering committee with the town and safeguarding the researchers' perceived legal requirements.

However, the reaction of the group was swift and unequivocal. Every one of the nine estate residents present, the entire steering group, totally opposed the presence of the police on the steering group. Despite their slight misunderstanding of our intent, they were entirely unanimous and steadfast regarding both the importance of the issue and the strength of their feeling about the matter.

One man described how the police had their own agenda, claiming all they contributed was delay and negativity and all they ever said was 'no'. Further, that they blocked all action and drove people away. He ended by announcing that if the police joined, he would immediately leave, and that, on past form, within a month, the entire steering group would have resigned.

No one disagreed or challenged this statement. In fact they unanimously endorsed it. The steering group understood that there was a fundamental difference in their mode of sociality and being-ness, which clashed with that of the police and the formal meanings they were tasked to enforce. This was thus an announcement stemming from a reflexive and actioned communal being-ness. It explicitly aimed to protect its own communal being-ness from what they unanimously viewed as a force dedicated to splitting and neutering that communal being-ness. For them, working *with* the police was impossible because the police wished only to work within a narrow framework that blocked anything that they might want to do. In this view, the police acted as a force to constrain and curtail and certainly not one to help and support.

Self-Policing

One of the most developed modes of social power is self-policing. There are complex debates about the legality of self-protection (e.g. attacking intruders), but the law specifically denies the capacity for independent communal formations to police themselves outside state jurisdiction.[3] Despite this, respondents reported many contemporary instances of self-policing on the estate. Indeed, respondents often seemed much more comfortable with this arrangement. Self-policing has much to teach us concerning sociality, communal being-ness and the implicit estate views about the effectiveness of police as a means for their own protection.

Earlier, we mentioned an account from a resident concerning a woman accused and convicted of child abuse who a government agency had relocated into the 'Deephollow' area of the estate.

His description continued thus:

Anyway she was moved in by protection order. And within an hour people knew exactly who she was and what she'd done. They'd gone round and started

---

[3] By independent here we mean totally outside any state control. Thus this excludes security licenced by the state to protect property or the person of private individuals.

in at her. Within three hours the police had taken her away and boarded up the windows on the house.

I: *It was that short?*
R: *No way shape or form once they get their teeth into a person will they let this person go*

The respondent goes on to say how he totally approved of this communal action.

I don't blame them. I got two kids. I don't want someone like that around either. No way.

For good or for bad, this outcome and the attitudes it drew upon were clearly the outcome of meanings-in-common and a communal being-ness shared by the entire area including those who took no direct role in the eviction. A less dramatic account of the self-policing on the estate was provided by another resident, H1.

She describes how in her section of Charlene Crescent ('its ok there— it's worse down the road') she has witnessed locals coming out onto the street at night-time to chastise boys making excessive noise and to be immediately joined by people from six other houses who had come out to lend their support and bolster communal being-ness.

She also described a recent situation in a house next door where there had been an ongoing, quite violent domestic dispute. The street had tolerated this dispute on eight previous occasions, but on the ninth occurrence, eight people had rung the police simultaneously. According to H1, the locals were always thrusting phone numbers into her hand: 'this is the number for the police', 'this is the social worker' or 'this is for the council.'

Lastly, the white van incident described in the earlier section also exists as an example of the communal being-ness of the estate acting in concert to protect itself. Field notes record that once the van was sighted, many in the office rushed outside to search of the van while those left inside immediately began ringing round, warning parents and friends. None of this appeared, as the field notes record, to be a practised behaviour.

Rather, it simply stemmed from an unspoken common agreement as to what was required.

Reading Communal Meanings

If we go back to the issue which began the chapter, that is, if we think about community policing from the point of view of communal being-ness, we begin to recognise that policing, for the estate at least, does not begin or end with the technologies of governance or the legal framework that comes with them.

Indeed, we argued that what made police embeddedness in Henry St work was less the rule of law and more the reinforcement of a form of authority designed to create a set of containing boundaries, supportive of communal being-ness in conditions that were difficult and at times threatening. Indeed, we saw from accounts of Henry Street that police never came into the space singularly, but always in threes and fours. Further that they 'negotiated' with the community for the handing over of people the community of Henry Street had themselves rejected.

On the estate, in the absence of physical proximity, coupled with the absence of police, embeddedness and containment, residents feel the need to protect themselves as best they can, using practices in which legality is not the foremost concern. Indeed, some residents go further than this and want professionals, including police to assist them in supporting and not leading them. That they seek a quite different approach to community policing from that of the police, is not in question.

When we consider the estate's views, we might pause to consider that people of property have always striven to protect themselves and their property beyond the confines and resources of the police. Just as the propertied protect their property with gated estates, security guards, insurance and burglar alarms, indeed with an entire industry dedicated to precisely that, and do not rely on the police, so in these instances described above, the actions of the estate acting through its own communal being-ness are understood by the estate as forms of self-protection within the limits of their available resources.

Self-policing is action in common. These examples of self-policing in contemporary Market-Town all present, in different forms, communal actions, stemming and, in turn, creative of, communal being-ness.

It is the action of being-ness, attending, in this case, to its own commonality and its own preservation. The police are a possible resource but they are not to be trusted; trust in this context meaning simply 'present'; present in a space of appearance sufficient to provide the community with safety.

This judgement passed upon the police is not an abstracted moral judgement or ungrounded 'fear', like 'fear of crime'. This judgement passed by the community upon the police is a meaning-in-common arising from the operational absence of police on the estate; simply put, for the residents the police do not deliver.[4]

Likewise, the self-policing practices in 'Deephollow' functioned as self defence against what the communal being-ness saw as an attack upon their children. This is clear in the support given to the action by our respondent.

In relation to this, one of the biggest issues, unspoken but nonetheless constantly present, is the difference between the emphasis attached by the estate to its own communal unity and being-ness as a means for solving problems affecting them and the perspective of the formal meanings of governance as these are expressed by the police and by other formal agencies.

The estate treasures its own communal being-ness because, fundamentally, it is its strongest resource. To that end, we saw how neighbours of H1 shared phone numbers for relevant authorities and hastened into the street to support each other against noisy gangs of youths idly roaming the estate at night-time on the weekend.

Thus, just as the communal being-ness is prepared to police itself, so it remains confident enough to initiate, or at least think up, programmes designed to help heal itself. Unfortunately, to date, it has never been felt even appropriate to ask their opinion, let alone allow them to run a programme of their choosing.

---

[4] Which makes an interesting conundrum for the Lockian state which promises, theoretically at least, to protect the citizen and guarantee their safety in exchange for that same citizen surrendering elements of their power to the state.

Bibliography

Baines, S., & Hardill, I. (2008). 'At least I can do something': The work of volunteering in a community beset by worklessness. *Social Policy and Society, 7,* 307–317. doi:10.1017/S1474746408004284.

Bick, E. (1968). The experience of skin in early object relations. *International Journal of Psychoanalysis, 49,* 484–486.

Evers, H.-D. (2003). Transition towards a knowledge society: Malaysia and Indonesia in comparative perspective. *Comparative Sociology, 2*(2), 355–373.

Hughes, G. (2007). *The politics of crime and community.* London: Palgrave.

Milligan, C., & Fyfe, N. R. (2004). Putting the voluntary sector in its place: Geographical perspectives on voluntary activity and social welfare in Glasgow. *Journal of Social Policy, 33*(1), 73–93. https://www.gov.uk/government/publications/building-the-big-society 2010

Portes, A. (1998). Social capital: Its origins and applications in modern sociology. *Annual Review of Sociology, 24,* 1–24.

Putnam, R., Leonardi, R., & Nanetti, R. (1993). *Making democracy work.* Princeton: Princeton University Press.

Roberts, J. M., & Devina, F. (2003). The hollowing out of the welfare state and social capita. *Social Policy and Society, 2,* 309–318.

Skogan, W. G. (1997). *Community policing Chicago style.* New York: Oxford University Press.

Young, J. (1999). *The exclusively society: Social exclusion, crime and difference in late modernity.* London: Sage.

9

Conclusion

Rethinking Community Research

We have taken the reader on a journey in which our approach to researching community differently was embedded in the streets of Market-Town itself. In concluding our book and our argument, we would like to consider the implications of our approach to investigation.

Chapter 1 investigated the background to social scientific research about community, critiquing the basis of present approaches, which understand community as an object, often one considered to be obsolete. Social science's obsession with the state/individual axis was discussed. The concept of a relationality in which communality can be rethought as an action of being in common was presented to the reader as a founding premise. The chapter also presented our research site, the town that we called Market-Town.

Chapter 2 developed the philosophical basis for our analytic and introduced the work of the political philosopher Hannah Arendt. It discussed

© The Author(s) 2016
D. Studdert, V. Walkerdine, *Rethinking Community Research*,
DOI 10.1057/978-1-137-51453-0_9

the concepts of sociality, inter-relationality, plurality, action and being-ness, while situating these within the streets of Market-Town.

Beginning by analysing an example of a track between a housing estate and the centre of the town, Chap. 3 demonstrated how it could be understood as a space of appearance, a place in which commonal-ity can be expressed. It developed further the analysis of the 'space of appearance' as a concept and considered, through a number of exam-ples from Market-Town, how plurality is achieved within the space of appearance.

The creation of being-ness through the production of meanings-in-common was the task of Chap. 4. Here, we were primarily interested in how a communal 'who' is created through the sharing of a sense of simi-larity of experience. To understand this, we considered several examples from the town, culminating in a discussion of the shared meaning of a much-loved local open-air swimming pool, closed by the council in the 1990s. By working through this example, we were also able to under-stand how meanings-in-common might be amplified to support com-munity development.

Hannah Arendt coined the term 'web of relations' to understand the overarching relationality in which all sociality is produced and moves, never still, constantly changing. Chap. 5 explored this and, in partic-ular, considered the relationship between the space of appearance and the web of relations. In considering how to study this web, the chapter engaged with a number of examples, especially considering the role of what could be called a 'moneyed web' within the town. This 'moneyed web' had a particular significance in that it was part of a historical trans-formation of Market-Town in which the centre and periphery of the town had been redefined. We showed that this historical transformation, also explored in Chap. 6, was not a simple shift in which everything recog-nised as community had ceased to exist, but rather, using the concepts of communal being-ness embedded in a web of relations, we found it possible to understand the complex ways in which communality changes form, but does not cease to exist.

In contrast to a moneyed web, Chap. 6 explored a moment in the town in which the centre of the town was fully inhabited by people who were later moved to its periphery on the estate. Considering the sociality that was present, the argument was developed that specific actions served to disperse this particular manifestation of the communal, but that does not mean that, despite it having been deliberately removed, communal being-ness ceases to exist where and when it can in the form that it is able. In particular, we discuss the ways in which what was once permitted on the streets is now confined to homes and exists online.

The concept of governmentality has become a well-known way to understand the role of governance and regulation in the production of what this book called being-ness. This issue was explored in Chap. 7. Work on governmentality generally assumes that it is the sole site for the production of subjects. This chapter considers the central importance of plurality, especially the relationship between those meanings produced through the discourses and practices of governance and those that circulate in informal meanings-in-common. In this way, the chapter takes the example of volunteering as it is used in current government policies and argues for an approach which considers how the government meanings rub up against those of the volunteers themselves, thus emphasising the importance of informal communal meanings.

The relationship between police and the communities they serve has shifted from more to less embedded and back again since the inception of formal police forces. Yet, academically, it is recognised that approaches to police–community relations from within the social sciences and criminology have attempted to understand the law and practices of policing, rather than engage with the meanings of policing for communities. Chapter 8 sought new ways of thinking about this by asking what it means to think about the meanings of policing as they circulate within Market-Town. By exploring policing in this way, the complex relationalities of community and police being-ness were revealed.

The Communal Being-ness of Market-Town

For us, thinking about community has meant coming to grips with the sociality productive of communal being-ness. We presented a communal being-ness stemming from Henry Street and the working past of the town, twinned with what we termed the 'moneyed web' centred around the Towers Hotel and the county and town councils. These two forms of communal being-ness are the ones most heavily invested in the shaping of Market-Town, vastly different though that shaping is. Nonetheless, jointly, they create its shape and space. They create its rituals, whether these be the annual town fest, the fights outside the disco, the boy-car racers on Saturday night or the shopping expeditions in Market-Town.

We discovered that Market-Town was composed of multiple actions of sociality, constructive of multiple being-nesses in common, that personal and communal being was held in multiple commonalities crossing a web of formal and informal relations lived simultaneously in all actions of sociality.

Thus, Market-Town for us was never one thing, as in 'the community of Market-Town' as a 1950s British study might have it.

Rather, it was the discovery of small continual actions of being-together taking place all over the town. We discovered tracks known only to certain groups, tracks up the hill, tracks through the Towers Hotel. We saw how all of these were constructive of being-ness in common through actions of sociality. We discovered the meanings these actions created and sustained. We discovered buildings and activities—spaces where these meanings were expressed, and the expression of them was cherished and remembered.

What we saw, above all, was that communal meanings existed. That communal being-ness, the things that are this static noun, community, are never static but fluid, inter-relational and not reducible to arbitrary nominated essences. That action together required and obeyed complex relationalities of speech, movement, location and sociality.

Perhaps at this point we should point to what is not present in this book. There are multiple forms of communal being-ness in Market-Town-many other modes of communal being-ness of which we barely scratched the surface. The communal being-ness of the commuter section of town, as well as smaller groups not mentioned, of which there are numerous examples we did not have space to explore. Some of these modes are interesting in themselves and could certainly be studied using this analytic. We are thinking here, for instance, of the group of nurses from the Pacific Rim employed at the local hospital.

In this monograph, however, we centred our use of the analytic upon the two fulcrums mostly heavily invested in the communal being-ness of Market-Town as a space and intersection of sociality.

Now, of course, the people of Market-Town, like all contemporary human beings, stand in simultaneous, multiple, constant spaces of appearance and thus are subject to, and also holding, several forms of being-ness creation in common.

What interested us particularly, however, among these multiple ever-present spaces of appearance, which we all inhabit, was the particular space of appearance called Market-Town or 'my/this community'.

In Market-Town, both the estate and the moneyed web were engaged in quite different ways with the fate of the town. The Civic Society discussed and impacted the estate, and others ran pensioners' clubs and food kitchens, bus trips, a drop-in centre and various hobby and social groups.

We saw how these co-existing modes of communal being-ness, while bound by location, had very little else in common regarding the town the state of the town and the vision for the town.

The people of the town are almost unanimous in their criticism of the town and county councils, while the Civic Society and the councils also united around a particular version of the town. This vision permeated the structures of council decision-making regarding the town. We saw how in relation to the fate of the open-air pool, for example, these two meanings expressed themselves quite differently. We saw how the communal being-ness in Henry Street was enacted and re-enacted through memory, space and sociality; how likewise the county set and the Towers Hotel were productive of communal being-ness, communal meaning and social power. In both cases, we saw commonality being created through actions of sociality; we saw that commonality of holding produced communal being-ness and that, indeed, communal meanings, communal being-ness and social power were simultaneous processes contained in the action of common holding. In this sense, even to the smallest degree, every action of sociality was productive of social power to some extent.

We also could not help but notice how these modes of communal being-ness stood in inter-relation with other forms of communal being-ness and their social power. The estate, for instance, stood as a communal being-ness in circles of inter-relation with those being-ness created by and within government programmes, wars on poverty, concerns about community (which always seem to be only about poor communities), as well of course within the universal national circle of state legality and equality before the law, applicable, at least in theory, equally to everyone. The county and moneyed web stood in the policies of neo-liberalism, in circles of Hollywood and royalty, as well as being united under the banner of causes like tourism through the magic of branding. They had linkages—financial, historic and personal—into the wider communal being-ness of national government.

We saw how their communal being-ness, marked as it was by discretion, demarcation and unspoken concealment, carried over into the governance of Market-Town, expressing that concealment through demarcation, for instance. We saw how this vision constructed Market-Town and the space of the town through three different statutory bodies: the town council, the county local area body and the county council itself—a plethora of parties, even if they were all crammed with familiar faces. We saw how the focus of the county moneyed web as expressed through them, was locked into, and dominated by, the main shopping street and parking issues.

We saw how decisions of this 'council bloc' sought to simultaneously construct the people of the estate as consumers while also containing their use of the town's public space and painting them as someone else's problem.

In contrast, the communal being-ness of the other Market-Town was expressed in the frequent exhorting of the spirit of the town people and the beauty of the surrounding hills, in their friends, in their sense of safety and, most of all, in their common memory of a town where prosperity was available for everyone, through any number of means.

We saw how poverty entered into the production of the communal being-ness of the estate, which, allowing for the substitution of widescreen televisions for dirt floors, has remained a constant in their lives for almost 80 years. Indeed, lacking employment, and perhaps eating worse now, the estate may well be poorer than the residents grandparents were in Henry Street. Yet the more the town pushes them onto 'the reservation', while feeding off them as consumers, the more the estate clings to its own forms of communal safety and being-ness. The estate is excluded from the employment of the town, the spaces of the town and from the festivals that are celebrated in the town. They are not present in the displays in the town museum, or in the theatre; they feel unwelcome in the leisure centre and the town after dark. To many, the community of Market-Town appears to have shrunk to simply the main street.

Yet, efforts to create sustaining forms of communal being-ness were everywhere among many community groups. For example, the spirit we saw in the pensioners' lunches is a history of inter-relationality, linkage and being-ness in common as a means of survival. The pensioners' lunches were important to this communal being-ness as were the cheap food kitchens. All these sites action a sense of communal being-ness—of what their own community needed and how they wanted it provided. Yet in both these cases, the council closed and denuded these efforts. The reckless behaviour of town councils over the past 30 years in regard to the public social space of Market-Town is a strong theme running through accounts of Market-Town people. It figures in talk around certain symbols: the pool, the market, the main street.

The denial of communal space has, as all respondents agree, accelerated immensely over the last ten years. 'It's a dead town now.' Thus, what sustains communal being-ness, the construction of being-ness in common through the action of sociality, is denied a place to reveal itself. It is in this sense that we considered the ways in which, in the absence of social spaces to meet in the evenings, for example, online communities, such as the Facebook page, allowed a communal being-ness to survive in a different way.

When the council talks about 'the community' or tourist brochures do the same, we should recall that none of this denial of space, none of this repressed social being-ness features or appears. That it is precisely these elements which are disqualified and concealed.

This analytic attempts to move us beyond notions of 'community of location', community as a noun or phrases such as 'the community of Market-Town'. Instead, it offers an analysis, stressing the simultaneous production of webs of relationalities produced from all relations of communal being. We thus propose this approach as a way past attempts to critique 'community' as an object or to provide theoretical substitutions such as 'network', 'civil society', while proposing that it offers a productive method for examining our own sociality and our place in it.

Social Power

Throughout the book, we have referred to the term 'social power'. Communal being-ness is expressed through action; this action could be called social power. In the book, we gave examples such as the pensioners' centre with its lunches, the attempt to set up a community drop-in centre, or the group making cheap and healthy lunches in the leisure centre. There are countless other examples. We also discussed the Civic Society and its social power.

Thus by viewing sociality and communal being-ness inter-relationally, we were also able to think in a different way about power: how it works, how it exists in social formations.

Thinking inter-relationally allows us to identify social power as an outcome of a specific communal being-ness. Through sociality and being-ness in common we can understand power as it is expressed through the terms of social action and containment within infinite spaces of appearance. This presents some added complexity to understandings of governance as a micro-physics of power. While governance is everywhere, as we have witnessed, it does always meet, and can be contested by, other forms of communal being-ness. While the state claims to be the sole source of all communal being-ness by asserting its sovereignty in the construction of being-ness in common, especially a form of being-ness that stresses the actions of a single individual or family unit, other meanings are asserted, as we demonstrated with both volunteering and policing on the estate. So when the estate volunteers ask to work in their own way or when the posters on Facebook share photos of Henry St, their bodies share those which have been pushed and continue to be pushed, to the margins of the social by the liberal project. Those demands and meanings define the actuality of a social power not contained by the micro-physics of governmentality.

When the meaning-in-common of the volunteers or estate demands for self-policing surface, they share common ground with other initiatives that may have lasted 60 years (the pensioners' centre) or less than a year (the food kitchen), or they may have been accepted by the state only to be forced into a straightjacket not originally intended (the drop-in centre). All can be understood as community examples of social power which oppose the practices of social power coming from the web of relation of governance. And this gets to the heart of what we have been attempting to express in this book. Of course, community views are often polled, but communal meanings, especially of the poor, pose a challenge to that form of state sociality that wishes to claim all sociality for itself.

As the examples presented in this book have demonstrated, social power can veer from what might be understood as progressive self-help and local empowerment, to what is feared as vigilantism. Our approach proposes that it is the ignoring of attempts at producing meanings-in-common, acting within historically and culturally specific spaces of appearance, that emerge within particular local, national and international conditions of possibility, that either facilitate attempts to support communality or thwart it. The so-called vigilantism of the response to an abuser being brought to live on the estate can be understood as a result of experiences of lack of safety on the one hand and the lack of any kind of recognition by the police or other apparatuses of governance on the other. The blocking responses to local initiatives, in the face of sustained attempts to innovate on the part of local people, lead to a lack of trust and interest in what the state might actually do for local people, what agendas it puts in place and what prices it exacts for participation.

What the social sciences has understood as the demise of community and the dominance of a liberal project, governing only through a relation between a micro-physics of power and an individual, it has mistaken for the destruction of communal being-ness as a social form and force.

As we have begun to articulate, communal being-ness exists, but its existence and its demands challenge liberalism and the rule of law. It challenges governments not to treat people as isolated, passive victims, but as part of a constantly moving set of relational linkages that take their being-ness from each other, that we might call social power.

We are not therefore suggesting that understanding social power as an outcome of communal being-ness is a straightforward or easy option, but we argue that the issue itself must be understood and faced in the current historical context. In understanding the mixture of drugs, crime, protection and vigilantism in Deep Hollow, for example, we need to also grasp the ways that people try to live together, the ways in which they protect their children, make a living and support each other. This is a complex sociality in which the communal being-ness created must be understood within the space of appearance that makes it possible.

Failure to engage with this, to understand its provenance and to recognise its complexities as social power, does no service to anyone. In this analysis, it is unhelpful to support one set of actions as empowerment and condemn others as reactionary. That kind of moralism is unhelpful but it has dogged other approaches to community research. We could argue that many suspicions about 'community' as a concept come from a deep ambivalence about this place and an uncertainty about how to understand and to engage with it politically. We argue that only a fundamental rethinking of these issues will help us move forward in a way that can productively engage with the challenging complexities of the current geopolitical context.

References

Adam, B., Beck, U., & Van Loon, J. (2000). *The risk society and beyond*. London: Sage.

Agamben, G. (1999). Transcript Daniel Heller-Roazen. *Homo Sacer: Sovereign power & the bare life*. Stanford, CA: Stanford University Press.

Allan, G., & Crow, G. (2001). *Families, households and society* (pp. xl + 246). Basingstoke and London: Palgrave.

Alpert, G. P., & Piquero, A. R. (2000). *Community policing: Contemporary readings*. Illinois: Waveland Press.

Althusser, B. (1971). *Lenin & philosophy & other essays*. London: New Left Books.

Appadurai, A. (Ed.). (1986). *The social life of things*. Cambridge: Cambridge University Press.

Arendt, H. (1961). *Between past and future*. London: Faber and Faber.

Arendt, H. (1968). *Totalitarianism*. New York: Harcourt, Bruce & World.

Arendt, H. (1978). *The life of the mind*. London: Secker & Warberg.

Atkinson, D. (1994). *The common sense of community*. London: Demos.

Auge, M. (1995). *Non-places: Introduction to an anthropology of supermodernity* (trans: Howe, J.). London: Verso.

Auge, M. (1998). *A sense of the other*. Stanford: Stanford University Press.

© The Author(s) 2016   **221**
D. Studdert, V. Walkerdine, *Rethinking Community Research*,
DOI 10.1057/978-1-137-51453-0

Bauman, Z. (1992). *Intimation of post-modernity.* London: Routledge.

Bauman, Z. (2001a). *Community: Seeking safety in an insecure world.* Cambridge: Polity.

Bauman, Z. (2001b, April–June). The great war of recognition. *Theory Culture & Society,* 18(2–3).

Beck, U., Anthony, G., & Lash, S. (1994). *Reflexive modernization.* Cambridge: Polity Press.

Benhabib, S. (1992). *Situating the self.* Cambridge: Polity.

Benhabib, S. (1996). *The reluctant modernism of Hannah Arendt.* Thousand Oaks: Sage.

Benhabib, S., & Cornell, D. (Eds.). (1987). *Feminism as critique.* Cambridge: Polity Press.

Bhabha, H. K. (1994). *The location of culture.* London: Routledge.

Bird, J., Curtis, B., Putnam, T., Robertson, G., & Tickner, L. (Eds.). (1993). *Mapping the future.* London: Routledge.

Black, A. (Ed.). (1990). Community in historical perspective – A translation of selections from Das deutsche Genossensch-aftsrecht (The German Law of Fellowship) by von Gierke, O. Cambridge: Cambridge University Press.

Butler, J., Laclau, E., & Zizek, S. (2000). *Contingency, hegemony, universality.* London: Verso.

Calhoune, C. (1997). Plurality promises and the public spaces. In Calhoune, C. & J. McGowan (Eds.), *Hannah Arendt and the meaning of politics.* Minneapolis: University of Minnesota Press.

Calhoune, C., & McGowan, J. (1997). Hannah Arendt & the meaning of politics. In Calhoune, C. & J. McGowan (Eds.), *Hannah Arendt & the meaning of politics.* Minneapolis: University of Minnesota Press.

Cascardi, A. J. (1997). Communication and transformation: Aesthetics & politics in Kant and Arendt. In Calhoune, C. & J. McGowan (Eds.), *Hannah Arendt and the meaning of politics.* Minneapolis: University of Minnesota Press.

Castells, M. (1998). *End of millennium.* Oxford: Blackwell.

Castells, M. (2000). *The rise of the network society.* Oxford: Blackwell.

Castells, M. (2002). *The Internet Galaxy: Reflections on the Internet, Business, and Society.* Oxford: Oxford University Press.

Chambers, S. C. (1999). *From subjects to citizens.* Philadelphia: Pennsylvania State University Press.

Cincinnah, A. (2002). *Community policing: A contemporary perspective.* Cincinnati: Anderson.

Cohen, A. (1981). *The politics of elite culture.* Berkeley: University of California Press.

Crow, G. (1997). *Comparative sociology and social theory: Beyond the three worlds* (pp. viii + 206). Basingstoke and London: Macmillan.

Crow, G., & Allan, G. (1994). *Community life: An introduction to local social relations* (pp. xxv + 229). Hemel Hempstead: Harvester Wheatsheaf.

Curtis, K. (1997). Aesthetic foundations of democratic politics in the work of Hannah Arendt. In Calhoune, C. & J. McGowan (Eds.), *Hannah Arendt and the meaning of politics.* Minneapolis: University of Minnesota.

Darwin. (2009 [1892]) *On the origin of species by means of natural selection.* London: General Books.

Dean, M. (1994). *Critical and effective histories: Foucault's methods and historical sociology.* London: Routledge.

Dean, M. (1999). *Govermentality, power and rule in modern society.* London: Sage.

Deep maps: Liminal histories and the located imagination. *Journal of the Imaginary and Fantastic, 2*(4).

De Landa (2002). A new ontology for the social sciences, presented at Transdisciplinary Objects, University of Illinois.

Digeser, P. (1995). *Our politics ourselves?: Liberalism, identity and harm.* Princeton: Princeton University Press.

Dumont, L. (1980). *Homo Hierarchicus.* Chicago: University of Chicago Press.

Elias, N. (1974). Towards a theory of communities. In C. Bell & H. Newby (Eds.), *The sociology of community: Selection of readings.* London: Frank Cass and Co.

Featherstone, M. (Ed.). (1992). *Cultural theory & cultural change.* London: Sage.

Fenton, S., Rainer, R., & Hammett, I. (1984). *Durkheim and modern sociology.* Cambridge: Cambridge University Press.

Fraser, N. (2001). Recognition without ethics. *Theory Culture & Society, 18*(2 & 3), 21–43.

Giddens, A. (1971). *Capitalism & modern social theory.* Cambridge: Cambridge University Press.

Giddens, A. (1992). *The transformation of intimacy.* Cambridge: Polity Press.

Giddens, A. (1994). *Beyond left and right.* Cambridge: Polity Press.

Greene, J. R., & Mastrofski, D. (Eds.). (1991). *Community policing rhetoric or reality.* New York: Praeger.

Harre, R. (1998). When the knower is also the known. In May, T. & M. Williams (Eds.), *Knowing the social world.* Philadelphia: Open University Press.

Harre, R. (1999). Trust and its surrogates: Psychological foundations of political process. In M. E. Warren (Ed.), *Democracy and trust*. Cambridge: Cambridge University Press.

Held, D. (1989). *Political theory and the modern state*. Stanford: Stanford University Press.

Heller, A. (1984). *Everyday life*. London: Routledge.

Heller, A., & Feher, F. (1988). *The post modern political condition*. Cambridge: Polity Press.

Honig, B. (1993). *Political theory and the displacement of politics*. Ithaca: Cornell University Press.

Honneth, A. (1995). *The struggle for recognition: The moral grammar of social conflict* (trans: Anderson, J.). Cambridge: Polity Press.

Honneth, A. (2000). *Suffering from indeterminacy* (trans: Ben-Levi, J.). Van Gorcum, Department of Philosophy University of Amsterdam.

Hope, T. (1995). Community crime prevention. In M. Tonry & D. P. Farrington (Eds.), *Building a safer society – Strategic approaches to crime prevention* (Vol. 19). Chicago: University of Chicago Press.

Hughes, P., Bellamy, J., & Black, A. (2000). Building social trust through education. In Winter, I. (Ed.), *Social capital & public policy in Australia*. Melbourne: Australian Institute of Family Studies.

Keane, J. (1988). *Democracy and civil society*. London: University of Westminister Press.

Kynan, G. (2013). *History, heritage and localism policy studies*. Volume Special Issue: Understanding Localism, Part 2. 34, Issue 5–6, 2013.

Lash, S. (1999). *Another modernity, a different rationality*. Oxford: Blackwell.

Law, J., & Hassard, J. (1999). *Actor network theory and after*. London: Blackwell.

Lefort, C. (1988). *Democracy & political theory*. Minneapolis: University of Minnesota Press.

Matthews, R., & John, P. (2001). *Crime disorder and community safety*. London: Routledge.

Miller, J. (1979). Hannah Arendt's conception of the political community. In H. Melvyn A (Ed.), *Hannah Arendt, the recovery of the public world*. New York: St. Martins Press.

O'Byrne, D. (1997). Working class culture: Local community and global relations. In J. Eade (Ed.), *Living the global city: Globalisation as a local process*. London: Routledge.

Outhwaite, W. (1994). *Habermas: A critical introduction*. Stanford: Stanford University Press.

Pawson, R. (2013). *The science of evaluation: A realist manifesto.* London: Sage.

Pitkin, H. F. (1998). *The attack of the blob: Hannah Arendt's concept of the social.* Chicago: University of Chicago Press.

Portes, A. (2000). Social capital: Its origins & applications in modern sociology. In Lesser, E. R. (Ed.), *Knowledge & social capital.* Boston: Butterworth and Heinemann.

Putnam, R. D. (Ed.). (2002). *Democracies in flux.* Oxford: Oxford University Press.

Putnam, R. D., Leonardi, R., & Nanetti, R. Y. (1993). *Making democracy work.* Princeton: Princeton University Press.

Rosanvallon, P. (1988). The decline of social visibility. In Keane, J. (Ed.), *Civil society and the state: New European perspectives.* London: Verso.

Savage, M. (2015). *Social class in the 21st century.* London: Pelican.

Seligman, A. B. (1992). *The idea of civil society.* New York: The Free Press.

Selznick, P. (1992). *The moral commonwealth.* Berkeley: University of California Press.

Sennett, R. (1998). *The corrosion of character.* New York: Norton.

Serageldin, S., & Grootaert, C. (2000). Defining social capital: An integrating view. In Dasgupta, P. (Ed.), *Social capital: A multi -faceted perspective.* World Bank.

Skolnick, J. H. (2011). *Justice without trial: Law enforcement in democratic society.* New Orleans: Quid Pro Books.

Smith, D. E. (1987). *The everyday world as problematic.* Boston: North Western University Press.

Sullivan, W. (1990). *Re-inventing community: Prospects for politics.* New York: New York Press.

Uslaner, E. M. (1999). Democracy & social capital. In Warren, M. (Ed.), *Democracy and trust.* Cambridge: Cambridge University Press.

Uslaner, E. M. (2002). *The moral foundations of trust.* Cambridge: Cambridge University Press.

Venn, C. (2000). *Occidentalism: Modernity & subjectivity.* London: Sage.

Villa, D. R. (1987). Hannah Arendt: Modernity, alienation & critique. In Calhoune, C. & J. McGowan (Eds.), *Hannah Arendt and the meaning of politics.* Minneapolis: University of Minnesota Press.

Villa, D. R. (1999). *Politics, philosophy & terror: Essays on the thought of Hannah Arendt.* Princeton: Princeton University Press.

Villa, D. (Ed.). (2000). *The Cambridge companion to Hannah Arendt.* Cambridge: Cambridge University Press.

Walkerdine, V. (2006). *Public lecture: ESRC identities series, minding the gap: Thinking subjectivity beyond a psychic/discursive division*. University of the West of England.

Waterton, E., & Watson, S. (Eds.). (2015). *The Palgrave handbook of contemporary heritage research*. London: Palgrave.

Wetherall, M. (Ed.). (2009). *Theorizing identities and social action*. London: Palgrave Macmillan.

Wittel, A. (2001, December). Towards a network sociality. *Theory, Culture & Society, 18*(6).

Young, J. (1999a). *The exclusively society: Social exclusion, crime and difference in late modernity*. London: Sage.

Young, I. M. (1999b). Justice, inclusion, and deliberative democracy. In Maceo, S. (Ed.), *Deliberative politics: Essays on democracy and disagreement*. Oxford: Oxford University Press.

Index

© The Author(s) 2016   **227**
D. Studdert, V. Walkerdine, *Rethinking Community Research*,
DOI 10.1057/978-1-137-51453-0

Made in the USA
Monee, IL
15 March 2021

62867425R00138